Based on the Terry Lectures
delivered at Yale University

EDUCATION AT THE CROSSROADS

EDUCATION
AT THE
CROSSROADS

BY

JACQUES MARITAIN

NEW HAVEN AND LONDON
YALE UNIVERSITY PRESS

ISBN: 0-300-00163-0 (paper)

Printed in the United States of America.

41   40   39

PREFACE

Education at the Crossroads appeared in 1943. The present paperbound edition has been prepared directly from the original printed text, and it was therefore impossible for me to bring the book up to date. It was written during the Second World War. I beg the reader to be kind enough to remember this fact, so as not to be taken aback by allusions to "the present war", or by considerations relating to the problem of post-war Germany which the course of events has caused to seem rather naïve today—though at least they remind us of the serious questions which faced the Western world at the time of the war against Hitler.

As I wrote in the Acknowledgment of the original edition, I am deeply appreciative of the honor that Yale University conferred upon me in inviting me to give the Terry Lectures for 1943. And I should like to express here my gratitude.

I am particularly indebted to Professor and Mrs. Charles W. Hendel, for the thoughtful and invaluable coöperation they gave me in the final drafting of these lectures. I am also indebted to Dr. Gerald B. Phelan, with whom I had the privilege of discussing many problems involved while I was preparing part of the present volume at the Pontifical Institute of Mediaeval Studies of Toronto; and to my American friends who helped me in revising the text and the proofs. When I read years ago *The Higher Learning in America*, by Dr. Robert M. Hutchins, then President of the University of Chicago, I did not dream I should one day have to discuss such educational topics in this country, at a time of supreme emergency. I am particularly pleased to pay tribute here to Dr. Hutchins' work and books.

May I finally offer my sincere thanks to the professors

and students of Yale University, and to the audience which attended the lectures, for the cordial and generous encouragement I received from them.

JACQUES MARITAIN

Princeton, January 1960

CONTENTS

PREFACE   v

I. THE AIMS OF EDUCATION   1

    1. The Nature of Man and Education   1
      The Education of Man, 1.—The First Misconception:
      a Disregard of Ends, 2.—The Second Misconception:
      False Ideas Concerning the End, 4.—The Scientific
      and the Philosophical-Religious Idea of Man, 4.—
      The Christian Idea of Man, 6.—Human Personality,
      7.—Personality and Individuality, 9.

    2. Concerning the Aims of Education   10
      The Conquest of Internal Freedom, 10.—The Third
      Misconception: Pragmatism, 12.—The Social Poten-
      tialities of the Person, 14.—The Fourth Misconcep-
      tion: Sociologism, 15.—The Fifth Misconception:
      Intellectualism, 18.—The Sixth Misconception: Vol-
      untarism, 20.

    3. The Paradoxes of Education   22
      The Seventh Misconception: Everything Can Be
      Learned, 22.—The Educational and Extra-educa-
      tional Spheres, 24.—The Educational System with
      Regard to the Formation of the Will and the Dignity
      of the Intellect, 25.

II. THE DYNAMICS OF EDUCATION   29

    1. The Dynamic Factors   29
      The Pupil's Mind and the Art of the Teacher, 29.—
      Education by the Rod and Progressive Education,
      31.—The True and the False Freeing of Personality,
      33.

    2. The Fundamental Dispositions To Be Fostered   36
      With Regard to Truth and Justice, 36.—With Re-
      gard to Existence, 37.—With Regard to Work, 38.—
      With Regard to the Others, 38.

    3. The Fundamental Norms of Education   39
      The First Rule, 39.—The Second Rule, 39.—The
      Freeing of the Intuitive Power, 42.—The Third Rule,
      45.—Spiritual Unity and Wisdom, 47.—The Fourth
      Rule, 49.—Knowledge and Training, 51.—The Inner
      Structure of the Curriculum, 55.

III. THE HUMANITIES AND LIBERAL EDUCATION   58

1. The Rudiments   58
The Spheres of Knowledge, 58.—The Child, 60.

2. The Humanities   61
The Adolescent, 61.—The Universal Character of
Liberal Education, 64.—The Curriculum, 66.—Phi-
losophy and Theology, 71.

3. The University   75
The Architecture of an Ideal University, 75.—The
Consummation of Liberal Education, 79.—The Insti-
tutes of Advanced Research, 83.—The Schools in
Spiritual Life, 84.—Our Responsibility toward
Youth, 86.

IV. THE TRIALS OF PRESENT-DAY EDUCATION   88

1. Liberal Education and the New Humanism
We Hope For   88
An Integral Education for an Integral Humanism,
88.—Human Leisure and Liberal Education, 89.

2. Some Special Tasks Imposed upon Education
with Regard to the World of Tomorrow   91
The Normal Task of Education and Its Superadded
Burdens, 91.—The Educational System and the State,
92.—Moral Teaching, 93.—The Needs of the Political
Commonwealth and Education, 97.

3. The Educational Problems Raised by the
Present World Crisis of Civilization   103
How to Remedy the Mental Perversion Brought
about by "Education for Death," 103.—Preventive
or Protective Measures, 104.—Constructive Work,
107.—About Europe, 109.—The Renewed Inspiration of Our Own Education, 113.

INDEX   119

I

THE AIMS OF EDUCATION

1. THE NATURE OF MAN AND EDUCATION

The Education of Man

THE general title I have chosen is *Education at the Crossroads*. I might also have entitled these chapters *The Education of Man*, though such a title may unintentionally seem provocative: for many of our contemporaries know primitive man, or Western man, or the man of the Renaissance, or the man of the industrial era, or the criminal man, or the bourgeois man, or the working man, but they wonder what is meant when we speak of man.

Of course the job of education is not to shape the Platonist man-in-himself, but to shape a particular child belonging to a given nation, a given social environment, a given historical age. Yet before being a child of the twentieth century, an American-born or European-born child, a gifted or a retarded child, this child is a child of man. Before being a civilized man—at least I hope I am—and a Frenchman nurtured in Parisian intellectual circles, I am a man. If it is true, moreover, that our chief duty consists, according to the profound saying of the Greek poet, Pindar, in *becoming who we are*, nothing is more important for each of us, or more difficult, than *to become a man*. Thus the chief task of education is above all to shape man, or to guide the evolving dynamism through which man forms himself as a man. That is why I might have taken for my title *The Education of Man*.

We shall not forget that the word education has a triple

yet intermingled connotation, and refers either to any process whatsoever by means of which man is shaped and led toward fulfilment (education in its broadest sense), or to the task of formation which adults intentionally undertake with regard to youth, or, in its strictest sense, to the special task of schools and universities.

In the present chapter I shall discuss the aims of education. In the course of this discussion we are to meet and examine, by the way, some significant misconceptions regarding education—seven of them in all.

Man is not merely an animal of nature, like a skylark or a bear. He is also an animal of culture, whose race can subsist only within the development of society and civilization, he is a *historical* animal: hence the multiplicity of cultural or ethico-historical patterns into which man is diversified; hence, too, the essential importance of education. Due to the very fact that he is endowed with a knowing power which is unlimited and which nonetheless only advances step by step, man cannot progress in his own specific life, both intellectually and morally, without being helped by collective experience previously accumulated and preserved, and by a regular transmission of acquired knowledge. In order to reach self-determination, for which he is made, he needs discipline and tradition, which will both weigh heavily on him and strengthen him so as to enable him to struggle against them—which will enrich that very tradition—and the enriched tradition will make possible new struggles, and so forth.

The First Misconception: a Disregard of Ends

Education is an art, and an especially difficult one. Yet it belongs by its nature to the sphere of ethics and practical wisdom. Education is an *ethical* art (or rather a practical wisdom in which a determinate art is embodied). Now every art is a dynamic trend toward an object to be achieved, which is the aim of this art. There is no art without ends, art's very vitality is the energy with which it tends toward its end, without stopping at any intermediary step.

Here we see from the outset the two most general misconceptions against which education must guard itself. The first misconception is a lack or disregard of ends. If means are liked and cultivated for the sake of their own perfection, and not as means alone, to that very extent they cease to lead to the end, and art loses its practicality; its vital efficiency is replaced by a process of infinite multiplication, each means developing and spreading for its own sake. This supremacy of means over end and the consequent collapse of all sure purpose and real efficiency seem to be the main reproach to contemporary education. The means are not bad. On the contrary, they are generally much better than those of the old pedagogy. The misfortune is precisely that they are so good that we lose sight of the end. Hence the surprising weakness of education today, which proceeds from our attachment to the very perfection of our modern educational means and methods and our failure to bend them toward the end. The child is so well tested and observed, his needs so well detailed, his psychology so clearly cut out, the methods for making it easy for him everywhere so perfected, that the end of all these commendable improvements runs the risk of being forgotten or disregarded. Thus modern medicine is often hampered by the very excellence of its means: for instance, when a doctor makes the examination of the patient's reactions so perfectly and carefully in his laboratory that he forgets the cure; in the meantime the patient may die, for having been too well tended, or rather analyzed. The scientific improvement of the pedagogical means and methods is in itself outstanding progress. But the more it takes on importance, the more it requires a parallel strengthening of practical wisdom and of the dynamic trend toward the goal.

The Second Misconception: False Ideas concerning the End

The second general error or misconception of education does not consist of an actual dearth of appreciation of the end but false or incomplete ideas concerning the nature of this end. The educational task is both greater and more mysterious and, in a sense, humbler than many imagine. If the aim of education is the helping and guiding of man toward his own human achievement, education cannot escape the problems and entanglements of philosophy, for it supposes by its very nature a philosophy of man, and from the outset it is obliged to answer the question: "What is man?" which the philosophical sphinx is asking.

The Scientific and the Philosophical-Religious Idea of Man

I should like to observe at this point that, definitely speaking, there are only two classes or categories of notions concerning man which play fair, so to speak: the purely scientific idea of man and the philosophical-religious one. According to its genuine methodological type, the scientific idea of man, like every idea recast by strictly experimental science, gets rid as far as possible of any ontological content, so that it may be entirely verifiable in sense-experience. On this point the most recent theorists of science, the neopositivists of the school of Vienna, are quite right. The purely scientific idea of man tends only to link together measurable and observable data taken as such, and is determined from the very start not to consider anything like being or essence, not to answer any question like: Is there a soul or isn't there? Does the spirit exist or only matter? Is there freedom or determinism? Purpose or chance? Value or simple fact? For such questions are out of the realm of science. The purely scientific idea of man is, and must be, a phenomenalized idea without reference to ultimate reality.

The philosophical-religious idea of man, on the contrary, is an ontological idea. It is not entirely verifiable in sense-experience, though it possesses criteria and proofs of its own, and it deals with the essential and intrinsic, though not visible or tangible characters, and with the intelligible density of that being which we call man.

Now it is obvious that the purely scientific idea of man can provide us with invaluable and ever-growing information concerning the means and tools of education, but by itself it can neither primarily found nor primarily guide education, for education needs primarily to know what man *is*, what is the nature of man and the scale of values it essentially involves; and the purely scientific idea of man, because it ignores "being-as-such," does not know such things, but only what emerges from the human being in the realm of sense observation and measurement. Young Tom, Dick, or Harry, who are the subjects of education, are not only a set of physical, biological, and psychological phenomena, the knowledge of which is moreover thoroughly needed and necessary; they are the children of man—this very name "man" designating for the common sense of parents, educators, and society the same ontological mystery as is recognized in the rational knowledge of philosophers and theologians.

It should be pointed out that if we tried to build education on the single pattern of the scientific idea of man and carry it out accordingly, we could only do so by distorting or warping this idea: for we should have to ask what is the nature and destiny of man, and we should be pressing the only idea at our disposal, that is the scientific one, for an answer to our question. Then we would try, contrary to its type, to draw from it a kind of metaphysics. From the logical point of view, we would have a spurious metaphysics disguised as science and yet deprived of any really philosophical insight; and from the practical point of view, we would have a denial or misconception of those very realities and values without which education loses all human sense or becomes the training of an animal for the utility of the state.

Thus the fact remains that the complete and integral idea of man which is the prerequisite of education can only be a philosophical and religious idea of man. I say philosophical, because this idea pertains to the nature or essence of man; I say religious, because of the existential status of this human nature in relation to God and the special gifts and trials and vocation involved.

The Christian Idea of Man

There are many forms of the philosophical and religious idea of man. When I state that the education of man, in order to be completely well grounded, must be based upon the Christian idea of man, it is because I think that this idea of man is the true one, not because I see our civilization actually permeated with this idea. Yet, for all that, the man of our civilization *is* the Christian man, more or less secularized. Consequently we may accept this idea as a common basis and imply that it is to be agreed upon by the common consciousness in our civilized countries, except among those who adhere to utterly opposite outlooks, like materialistic metaphysics, positivism, or skepticism— I am not speaking here of Fascist and racist creeds, which do not belong at all in the civilized world.

Now such a kind of agreement is all that any doctrine in moral philosophy can be expected to have, for none can pretend actually to obtain the literal universal assent of all minds—not because of any weakness in objective proof but because of the weakness inherent in human minds.

There does exist, indeed, among the diverse great metaphysical outlooks, if they recognize the dignity of the spirit, and among the diverse forms of Christian creeds, or even of religious creeds in general, if they recognize the divine destiny of man, a community of analogy as concerns practical attitudes and the realm of action, which makes possible a genuine human coöperation. In a Judeo-Greco-Christian civilization like ours, this community of analogy, which extends from the most orthodox religious forms of thought to the mere humanistic ones, makes it possible for a Christian philosophy of education, if it is well founded and rationally developed, to play an inspiring part in the concert, even for those who do not share in the creed of its supporters. Be it added, by the way, that the term concert, which I just used, seems rather euphemistic with regard to our "modern philosophies of education," whose discordant voices have been so valuably studied in Professor Brubacher's book.*

In answer to our question, then, "What is man?" we may give the Greek, Jewish, and Christian idea of man: man as an animal endowed with reason, whose supreme dignity is in the intellect; and man as a free individual in personal relation with God, whose supreme righteousness consists in voluntarily obeying the law of God; and man as a sinful and wounded creature called to divine life and to the freedom of grace, whose supreme perfection consists of love.

Human Personality

From the philosophical point of view alone the main concept to be stressed here is the concept of human personality. Man is a person, who holds himself in hand by his in-

* Cf. John S. Brubacher, *Modern Philosophies of Education* (New York and London, 1939).

telligence and his will. He does not merely exist as a physical being. There is in him a richer and nobler existence; he has spiritual superexistence through knowledge and love. He is thus, in some way, a whole, not merely a part; he is a universe unto himself, a microcosm in which the great universe in its entirety can be encompassed through knowledge. And through love he can give himself freely to beings who are to him, as it were, other selves; and for this relationship no equivalent can be found in the physical world.

If we seek the prime root of all this, we are led to the acknowledgment of the full philosophical reality of that concept of the soul, so variegated in its connotations, which Aristotle described as the first principle of life in any organism and viewed as endowed with supramaterial intellect in man, and which Christianity revealed as the dwelling place of God and as made for eternal life. In the flesh and bones of man there exists a soul which is a spirit and which has a greater value than the whole physical universe. Dependent though he may be upon the slightest accidents of matter, the human person exists by virtue of the existence of his soul, which dominates time and death. It is the spirit which is the root of personality.

The notion of personality thus involves that of wholeness and independence. To say that a man is a person is to say that in the depth of his being he is more a whole than a part and more independent than servile. It is this mystery of our nature which religious thought designates when it says that the person is the image of God. A person possesses absolute dignity because he is in direct relationship with the realm of being, truth, goodness, and beauty, and with God, and it is only with these that he can arrive at his complete fulfillment. His spiritual fatherland consists of the entire order of things which have absolute value, and which reflect, in some manner, a divine Absolute superior to the world and which have a power of attraction toward this Absolute.

Personality and Individuality

Now it should be pointed out that personality is only one aspect or one pole of the human being. The other pole is—to speak the Aristotelian language—individuality, whose prime root is matter. The same man, the same entire man who is, in one sense, a person or a whole made independent by his spiritual soul, is also, in another sense, a material individual, a fragment of a species, a part of the physical universe, a single dot in the immense network of forces and influences, cosmic, ethnic, historic, whose laws we must obey. His very humanity is the humanity of an animal, living by sense and instinct as well as by reason. Thus man is "a horizon in which two worlds meet." Here we face that classical distinction between the *ego* and the *self* which both Hindu and Christian philosophies have emphasized, though with quite diverse connotations. I shall come back to this thought later on.

I should like to observe now that a kind of animal training, which deals with psychophysical habits, conditioned reflexes, sense-memorization, etc., undoubtedly plays its part in education: it refers to material individuality, or to what is not specifically human in man. But education is not animal training. The education of man is a human awakening.

Thus what is of most importance in educators themselves is a respect for the soul as well as for the body of the child, the sense of his innermost essence and his internal resources, and a sort of sacred and loving attention to his mysterious identity, which is a hidden thing that no techniques can reach. And what matters most in the educational enterprise is a perpetual appeal to intelligence and free will in the young. Such an appeal, fittingly proportioned to age and circumstances, can and should begin with the first educational steps. Each field of training, each school activity—physical training as well as elementary reading or the rudiments of childhood etiquette and morals—can be intrinsically improved and can outstrip its own immediate practical value through being *humanized* in this way by understanding. Nothing should be required of the child without an explanation and without making sure that the child has understood.

2. CONCERNING THE AIMS OF EDUCATION

We may now define in a more precise manner the aim of education. It is to guide man in the evolving dynamism through which he shapes himself as a human person—armed with knowledge, strength of judgment, and moral virtues—while at the same time conveying to him the spiritual heritage of the nation and the civilization in which he is involved, and preserving in this way the century-old achievements of generations. The utilitarian aspect of education—which enables the youth to get a job and make a living—must surely not be disregarded, for the children of man are not made for aristocratic leisure. But this practical aim is best provided by the general human capacities developed. And the ulterior specialized training which may be required must never imperil the essential aim of education.

Now in order to get a complete idea of the aim of education, it is necessary to take into closer consideration the human person and his deep natural aspirations.

The Conquest of Internal Freedom

The chief aspirations of a person are aspirations to freedom—I do not mean that freedom which is free will and which is a gift of nature in each of us, I mean that freedom which is spontaneity, expansion, or autonomy, and which we have to gain through constant effort and struggle. And what is the more profound and essential form of such a desire? It is the desire for inner and spiritual freedom. In this sense Greek philosophy, especially Aristotle, spoke of the independence which is granted to men by intellect and wisdom as the perfection of the human being. And the Gospel was to lift up human perfection to a higher level—a truly divine one—by stating that it consists of the perfection of love and, as St. Paul put it, of the freedom of those who are moved by the divine Spirit. In any case it is by the activities that the philosophers call "immanent"—because they perfect the very subject which exerts them, and are within it the supreme activities of internal achievement and superabundance—that the full freedom of independence is won. Thus the prime goal of education is the conquest of internal and spiritual freedom to be achieved by the individual person, or, in other words, his liberation through knowledge and wisdom, good will, and love.

At this point we must observe that the freedom of which we are speaking is not a mere unfolding of potentialities without any object to be grasped, or a mere movement for the sake of movement, without aim or objective to be attained. It is sheer nonsense to offer such a movement to man as constituting his glory. A movement without aim is just running around in circles and getting nowhere. The aim, here on earth, will always be grasped in a partial and imperfect manner, and in this sense, indeed, the movement is to be pursued without end. Yet the aim will somehow be grasped, even though partially. Moreover the spiritual activities of the human being are *intentional* activities, they tend by nature toward an object, an objective aim, which will measure and rule them, not materially and by means of bondage, but spiritually and by means of liberty, for the object of knowledge or of love is internalized by the activity itself of the intelligence and the will, and becomes within them the very fire of their perfect spontaneity. Truth—which does not depend on us but on *what is*—truth is not a set of ready-made formulas to be passively recorded, so as to have the mind closed and enclosed by them. Truth is an infinite realm—as infinite as being—whose wholeness transcends infinitely our powers of perception, and each fragment of which must be grasped through vital and purified internal activity. This conquest of being, this progressive attainment of new truths, or the progressive realization of the ever-growing and ever-renewed significance of truths already attained, opens and enlarges our mind and life, and really situates them in freedom and autonomy. And speaking of will and love rather than knowledge, no one is freer, or more independent, than the one who gives himself for a cause or a real being worthy of the gift.

The Third Misconception: Pragmatism

Here we find ourselves confronted with the inappropriateness of the pragmatic overemphasis in education— a third error or misconception that we meet on our path. Many things are excellent in the emphasis on action and "praxis," for life consists of action. But action and praxis aim at an object, a determining end without which they lose direction and vitality. And life exists, too, for an end which makes it worthy of being lived. Contemplation and self-perfection, in which human life aspires to flower forth, escape the purview of the pragmatic mind.

It is an unfortunate mistake to define human thought as an organ of response to the actual stimuli and situations of the environment, that is to say, to define it in terms of animal knowledge and reaction, for such a definition exactly covers the way of "thinking" proper only to animals without reason. On the contrary, it is because every human idea, to have a meaning, must attain in some measure (be it even in the symbols of a mathematical interpretation of phenomena), what things *are* or consist of unto themselves; it is because human thought is an instrument or rather a vital energy of knowledge or spiritual intuition. (I don't mean "knowledge about," I mean "knowledge into"); it is because thinking begins, not only with difficulties, but with *insights*, and ends up in insights which are made true by rational proving or experimental verifying, not by pragmatic sanction, that human thought is able to illumine experience, to realize desires which are human because they are rooted in the prime desire for unlimited good, and to dominate, control, and refashion the world. At the beginning of human action, insofar as it is human, there is truth, grasped or believed to be grasped for the sake of truth. Without trust in truth, there is no human effectiveness. Such is, to my mind, the chief criticism to be made of the pragmatic and instrumentalist theory of knowledge.

In the field of education, this pragmatic theory of knowledge, passing from philosophy to upbringing, can hardly produce in the youth anything but a scholarly skepticism equipped with the best techniques of mental training and the best scientific methods, which will be unnaturally used against the very grain of intelligence, so as to cause minds to distrust the very idea of truth and wisdom, and to give up any hope of inner dynamic unity.*
Moreover, by dint of insisting that in order to teach John mathematics it is more important to know John than to know mathematics—which is true enough in one sense—the teacher will so perfectly succeed in knowing John that

---

* The "four cults"—skepticism, presentism, scientism, anti-intellectualism—listed by Dr. Hutchins (*Education for Freedom* [1943], p. 35–36) are but offsprings of pragmatism's domination over education.

John will never succeed in knowing mathematics. Modern pedagogy has made invaluable progress in stressing the necessity of carefully analyzing and fixing its gaze on the human subject. The wrong begins when *the object to be taught* and *the primacy of the object* are forgotten, and when the cult of the means—not to an end, but without an end—only ends up in a psychological worship of the subject.

The Social Potentialities of the Person

I have spoken of the aspiration of the human person to freedom, and, first of all, to inner and spiritual freedom. The second essential form of this desire is the desire for freedom externally manifested, and this freedom is linked to social life and lies at its very root. For society is "natural" to man in terms not only of animal or instinctive nature but of human nature, that is, of reason and freedom. If man is a naturally political animal, this is so in the sense that society, required by nature, is achieved through free consent, and because the human person demands the communications of social life through the openness and generosity proper to intelligence and love as well as through the needs of a human individual born naked and destitute. Thus it is that social life tends to emancipate man from the bondage of material nature. It subordinates the individual to the common good, but always in order that the common good flow back upon the individuals, and that they enjoy that freedom of expansion or independence which is insured by the economic guarantees of labor and ownership, political rights, civil virtues, and the cultivation of the mind.

As a result, it is obvious that man's education must be concerned with the social group and prepare him to play his part in it. Shaping man to lead a normal, useful and coöperative life in the community, or guiding the develop-

ment of the human person in the social sphere, awakening
and strengthening both his sense of freedom and his sense
of obligation and responsibility, is an essential aim. But it
is not the primary, it is the secondary essential aim. The
ultimate end of education concerns the human person in
his personal life and spiritual progress, not in his relationship to the social environment. Moreover, with regard to
the secondary aim itself of which I am speaking, we must
never forget that personal freedom itself is as the core of
social life, and that a human society is veritably a group
of human freedoms which accept obedience and self-
sacrifice and a common law for the general welfare, in
order to enable each of these freedoms to reach in everyone a truly human fufillment. The man and the group are
intermingled with each other and they surpass each other
in different respects. Man finds himself by subordinating
himself to the group, and the group attains its goal only
by serving man and by realizing that man has secrets which
escape the group and a vocation which is not included in
the group.

The Fourth Misconception: Sociologism

Here we are confronted with a fourth error of misconception akin to the third one, which derives the supreme
rule and standard of education from social conditioning.
The essence of education does not consist in adapting a
potential citizen to the conditions and interactions of social
life, but first in *making a man*, and by this very fact in
preparing a citizen. Not only is it nonsense to oppose education for the person and education for the commonwealth,
but the latter supposes the former as a prerequisite, and in
return the former is impossible without the latter, for one
does not make a man except in the bosom of social ties
where there is an awakening of civic understanding and
civic virtues.

The old education is to be reproached for its abstract and bookish individualism. To have made education more experiential, closer to concrete life and permeated with social concerns from the very start is an achievement of which modern education is justly proud. Yet in order to reach completion such a necessary reform must understand, too, that to be a good citizen and a man of civilization what matters above all is the inner center, the living source of personal conscience in which originate idealism and generosity, the sense of law and the sense of friendship, respect for others, but at the same time deep-rooted independence with regard to common opinion. We must also understand that without abstract insight and intellectual enlightenment the more striking experiences are of no use to man, like beautiful colors in darkness; that the best way not to be bookish is to avoid textbooks as a plague, even textbooks in experientialism, but to read books, I mean to read them avidly; and to understand also that, in a more general way, the pursuit of concrete life becomes a decoy if it scatters the attention of man or child among practical trifles, psychotechnical recipes, and the infinity of utilitarian activities, while disregarding the genuine concrete life of the intellect and the soul. The sense of concrete reality is made blunt by utilitarianism; it develops and flowers forth through those activities which are all the more needed by human life since they are not at the service of any practical utility, because they are in themselves, freedom, fruit, and joy. Unfortunate is a youth who does not know the pleasure of the spirit and is not exalted in the joy of knowing and the joy of beauty, and enthusiasm for ideas, and quickening experience in the first love, delight and luxury of wisdom and poetry. Boredom and weariness with human affairs will come early enough indeed; to deal with them is the job of the grown-up.

To discuss the matter in a more specific manner, I should like to make the following observations: that conception which makes education itself a constantly renewed experiment, starting from the pupil's present purposes and developing in one way or another according to the success of his problem-solving activity with regard to these purposes and to new purposes arising from broadened experience in unforeseen directions, such a pragmatist conception has its own merits when it comes to the necessity of adapting educational methods to the natural interests of the pupil. But what are the standards for judging the purposes and values thus successively emerging in the pupil's mind? If the teacher himself has no general aim, nor final values to which all this process is related; if education itself is to grow "in whatever direction a novelly emerging future renders most feasible";* in other words, if the pragmatist theory requires a perpetual experimental reconstruction of the ends of the educator himself (and not only of the experience of the pupil), then it teaches educational recipes but gets away from any real art of education: for an education which does not have any goal of its own and tends only to growth itself without "end beyond further growth" † is no more an art than an art of architecture which would not have any idea of what is to be built, and would only tend to the growth of the construction in whatever direction a new addition of materials is feasible. In nature itself, biological growth is nothing but a morphological process, or the progressive acquisition of a definite form. And finally the pragmatist theory can only subordinate and enslave education to the trends which may develop in collective life and society, for in the last analysis the aims newly arising in such a "reconstruction of ends" will only be determined by the precarious factors of the

* Brubacher, *op. cit.*, p. 329.
† *Ibid.*

environment to be controlled and the values made at each moment predominant by given social conditions or tendencies or by the state.

The element of truth which must be preserved in the conception I have just discussed, is the fact that the final end of education—the fulfillment of man as a human person—is infinitely higher and broader than the aim of architectural art or even the aim of medical art, for it deals with our very freedom and spirit, whose boundless potentialities can be led to full human stature only by means of constant creative renewal. As a result, the vital spontaneity of the one to be educated plays a major part in the progress toward this final end, as well as the steady widening of the pupil's experience; and the need for constantly renewed adaptation of methods, means, and approaches is much greater in educational art than in any art dealing only with some material achievement.

The Fifth Misconception: Intellectualism

With regard to the powers of the human soul I should like now to indicate as briefly as possible two other errors which oppose one another and which come from overemphasis: intellectualism, the fifth error or misconception on our list; the other, voluntarism.

Intellectualism takes on two principal forms: a certain form of intellectualism seeks the supreme achievements of education in sheer dialectical or rhetorical skill—such was the case of classical pedagogy, especially in the bourgeois era, in which education was a privilege of privileged classes.

Another form of intellectualism, a modern one, gives up universal values and insists upon the working and experiential functions of intelligence. It seeks the supreme achievements of education in scientific and technical specialization. Now specialization is more and more needed by the technical organization of modern life, yet it should be compensated for by a more vigorous general training, especially during youth. If we remember that the animal is a specialist, and a perfect one, all of its knowing-power being fixed upon a single task to be done, we ought to conclude that an educational program which would only aim at forming specialists ever more perfect in ever more specialized fields, and unable to pass judgment on any matter that goes beyond their specialized competence, would lead indeed to a progressive animalization of the human mind and life. Finally, as the life of bees consists of producing honey, the real life of man would consist of producing in a perfectly pigeonholed manner economic values and scientific discoveries, while some cheap pleasure or social entertainment would occupy leisure time, and a vague religious feeling, without any content of thought and reality, would make existence a little less flat, perhaps a little more dramatic and stimulating, like a happy dream. The overwhelming cult of specialization dehumanizes man's life.

Fortunately, nowhere in the world has any educational system been set up solely on this basis. Yet there exists everywhere a trend toward such a conception of education, following a more or less conscious materialistic philosophy of life. This represents a great peril for the democracies, because the democratic ideal more than any other requires faith in and the development of spiritual energies—a field which is over and above any specialization—and because a complete division of the human mind and activities into specialized compartments would make impossible the very "government of the people, by the people, and for the people." How could the common man be capable of judging about the good of the people if he felt able to pass judgment only in the field of his own specialized vocational competence? Political activity and political judgment would become the exclusive job of specialized experts in the matter—a kind of state technocracy which does not open particularly felicitous perspectives either for the good of the people or for liberty. As for education—complemented by some imperative vocational guidance—it would become the regular process of differentiation of the bees in the human beehive. In reality, the democratic way of life demands primarily liberal education for all and a general humanistic development throughout society. Even as to industrial achievements, man's free ingenuity strengthened by an education which liberates and broadens the mind is of as great import as technical specialization, for out of these free resources of human intelligence there arises, in managers and workers, the power of adapting themselves to new circumstances and mastering them.

The Sixth Misconception: Voluntarism

Voluntarism, also, has two principal forms. In reaction against the first form of intellectualism, a voluntarist trend, developed since the time of Schopenhauer, has contributed to upset the internal order of human nature, by making intelligence subservient to the will and by appealing to the virtue of irrational forces. Accordingly, education was intended to concentrate either on the will which was to be disciplined according to some national pattern or on the free expansion of nature and natural potentialities. The merit of the best and wisest forms of voluntarism in the educational field * has been to call attention again to the essential importance of the voluntary functions, disregarded by intellectualist pedagogy, and to the primacy of morality, virtue, and generosity in the upbringing of man. For the main point is surely to be a good man rather than to be a learned man. As Rabelais put it, science without conscience is the ruin of the soul. Such was the ideal but in

* I am thinking for instance of the work of F. W. Foerster, whose influence has been great in many European pedagogical circles.

actual fact the pedagogic achievements of voluntarism have been strangely disappointing, at least from the point of view of the good. From the point of view of evil, they have had plenty of success—I mean in the effectiveness of Nazi training, schools, and youth organizations, in smashing all sense of truth in human minds and in perverting the very function of language and morally devastating the youth and making the intellect only an organ of the technical equipment of the state.

For the voluntarist trend in education combines very well with technical training. We find such a combination not only in the totalitarian corruption of education but elsewhere also, and there to some good purpose. As we see it in democratic countries, this peculiar form of educational voluntarism may be described as an effort to compensate for the inconveniences of the second form of intellectualism —overspecialized technical training—by what is known as education of will, education of feeling, formation of character, etc. Yet the misfortune is that this commendable effort has yielded, as a rule, the same disappointing result of which I spoke a moment ago.* Character is something easily warped or debased, difficult to shape. All the pedagogical hammering of nails into the shoe doesn't make the shoe more comfortable to the foot. The methods which change the school into a hospital for refitting and vitaliz-

* Voluntarism does not succeed in forming and strengthening the will, but it succeeds in deforming and weakening the intellect, by the very fact that it exaggerates the province of the will in thought itself, so as to make everything a matter of one's will to believe. It has been pointed out in this connection that "just as in the realm of politics, the primacy of will identifies authority with force, so in the realm of thought the primacy of will reduces everything to arbitrary opinions or academic conventions. There are no first truths, but only postulates, demands of the will that something be taken for granted. In some sense, all knowledge rests on acts of faith, though the only principle of such faith is one's private predilections." Mortimer J. Adler, "Liberalism and Liberal Education," *The Educational Record*, July, 1939, pp. 435–436.

ing the wills, suggesting altruistic behavior or infusing good citizenship, may be well conceived and psychologically suitable, but they are for the most part dishearteningly ineffective.

We believe that intelligence is in and by itself nobler than the will of man, for its activity is more immaterial and universal. But we believe also that, in regard to the things or the very objects on which this activity bears, it is better to will and love the good than simply to know it. Moreover it is through man's will, when it is good, not through his intelligence, be it ever so perfect, that man is made good and right. A similar intermingling of roles is to be found in education, taken in its broadest sense. The upbringing of the human being must lead both intelligence and will toward achievement, and the shaping of the will is throughout more important to man than the shaping of the intellect. Yet, whereas the educational system of schools and colleges succeeds as a rule in equipping man's intellect for knowledge, it seems to be missing its main achievement, the equipping of man's will. What an infelicity!

3. THE PARADOXES OF EDUCATION

The Seventh Misconception: Everything Can Be Learned

We are here confronted with some paradoxical aspects of education. The main paradox can be formulated as follows: what is most important in education is not the job of education, and still less that of learning. Here we face an error terribly current in the modern world—the seventh error or misconception on our list—which boils down to the belief that everything can be learned. Greek sophists, too, believed that everything, even virtue, could be gotten by means of learning and discussing the matter. It is not true that everything can be learned, and that youth must earnestly expect from colleges not only courses in cooking, housekeeping, nursing, advertising, cosmetology,* money-making, and getting married, but also—why not?—courses on the scientific means of acquiring creative genius in art or science, or of consoling those who weep, or of being a man of generosity.

The teaching of morality, with regard to its intellectual bases, should occupy a great place in school and college education. Yet that right appreciation of practical cases which the ancients called *prudentia*, and which is an inner vital power of judgment developed in the mind and backed up by well-directed will, cannot be replaced by any learning whatsoever. Nor can experience, which is an incommunicable fruit of suffering and memory, and through which the shaping of man is achieved, be taught by any school or any courses. There are courses in philosophy, but no courses in wisdom; wisdom is gained through spiritual experience, and as for practical wisdom, as Aristotle put it, the experience of old men is both as undemonstrable and illuminating as the first principles of understanding. Moreover, is there anything of greater import in the education of man than that which is of the greatest import for man and human life? For man and human life there is indeed nothing greater than intuition and love. Not every love is right, nor every intuition well directed or conceptualized, yet if either intuition or love exists in any hidden corner, life and the flame of life are there, and a bit of heaven in a promise. Yet neither intuition nor love is a matter of training and learning, they are gift and freedom. In spite of all that, education should be primarily concerned with them.† I shall come back to this point in my next

* "I attacked vocationalism, and the University of California announced a course in cosmetology, saying 'The profession of beautician is the fastest growing in this state.'" Robert M. Hutchins, *Education for Freedom* (Louisiana State University Press, 1943), p. 19.

† "Education ought to teach us how to be in love always and what to be in love with. The great things of history have been done by the great

chapter with regard to intuition. With regard to love, which is the soul of moral life, the whole problem of morality is involved, and I shall be able only to touch upon it occasionally.

The Educational and Extra-educational Spheres

Another paradox deals with what may be called the educational and extra-educational spheres. By educational spheres I mean those collective entities which have always been recognized as especially committed to educational training: namely the family, the school, the state, and the Church. Here the surprising thing is that on the one hand the family, which is the first and fundamental educational sphere, grounded in nature, performs its educational task while not infrequently making the child a victim of psychological traumatisms, or of the bad example, ignorance, or prejudice of the adult; and that on the other hand the school, whose special and vocational function is education, performs its educational task while not infrequently making the youth a victim of stupefying overwork or disintegrating chaotic specialization, and often extinguishing the fire of natural gifts and defrauding the thirst of natural intelligence by dint of pseudo-knowledge. The solution is surely not to get rid of the family or of the school, but to endeavor to make them more aware and more worthy of their call, to acknowledge not only the necessity of mutual help but also the inevitability of a reciprocal tension between the one and the other, and to recognize, too, that

lovers, by the saints and men of science and artists; and the problem of civilization is to give every man a chance of being a saint, a man of science, or an artist. But this problem cannot be attempted, much less solved, unless men desire to be saints, men of science, and artists, and if they are to desire that continuously and consciously, they must be taught what it means to be these things." Sir Arthur Clutton-Brock, *The Ultimate Belief* (New York, 1916), p. 123. Quoted by John U. Nef, *The United States and Civilization* (Chicago, 1942), p. 265.

from the very start, I say from childhood on, man's condition is to suffer from and defend himself against the most worthy and indispensable supporters whom maternal nature has provided for his life, and thus to grow amidst and through conflict, if only energy, love, and good will quicken his heart.

Yet what is perhaps most paradoxical is that the extra-educational sphere—that is, the entire field of human activity, particularly everyday work and pain, hard experiences in friendship and love, social customs, law (which is a "pedagogue," according to St. Paul), the common wisdom embodied in the behavior of the people, the inspiring radiance of art and poetry, the penetrating influence of religious feasts and liturgy—all this extra-educational sphere exerts on man an action which is more important in the achievement of his education than education itself. Finally the all-important factor is a transcendent one, that call of the hero which Henri Bergson so insistently emphasized, and which passes through the whole structure of social habits and moral regulations as a vitalizing aspiration toward the infinite Love which is the source of being. The saints and the martyrs are the true educators of mankind.

The Educational System with Regard to the Formation of the Will and the Dignity of the Intellect

We may now come back to the intermingling of intelligence and will of which I spoke earlier. We must here stress some characteristics of school and college education which are often insufficiently taken into account. School and college education is only a part of education. It pertains only to the beginnings and the completed *preparation* of the upbringing of man, and no illusion is more harmful than to try to push back into the microcosm of school education the entire process of shaping the human being, as if the system of schools and universities were a big factory through the back door of which the young child enters like a raw material, and from the front door of which the youth in his brilliant twenties will go out as a successfully manufactured man. Our education goes on until our death. Further, even in this preparatory field, school education itself has only a partial task, and this task is primarily concerned with knowledge and intelligence.

Teaching's domain is the domain of truth—I mean speculative as well as practical truth. The only dominating influence in the school and the college must be that of truth, and of the intelligible realities whose illuminating power obtains by its own virtue, not by virtue of the human authority of the master's say-so, the assent of an "open mind," intending to pronounce one way or another "according to the worth of evidence." No doubt the child's "open mind" is still unarmed, and unable to judge "according to the worth of evidence"; the child must believe his teacher. But from the very start the teacher must respect in the child the dignity of the mind, must appeal to the child's power of understanding, and conceive of his own effort as preparing a human mind to think for itself. The one who does not yet know must believe a master, but only in order to know, and maybe to reject at this very moment the opinions of the master; and he believes him provisionally, only because of the truth which the teacher is supposed to convey.

Thus it is chiefly through the instrumentality of intelligence and truth that the school and the college may affect the powers of desire, will, and love in the youth, and help him gain control of his tendential dynamism. Moral education plays an essential part in school and college education, and this part must be more and more emphasized. But it is essentially and above all by way of knowledge and teaching that school education must perform this moral task, that is to say, not by exercising and giving rectitude to the will—nor by merely illuminating and giving rectitude to speculative reason—but by illuminating and giving rectitude to practical reason. The forgetting of this distinction between *will* and *practical reason* explains the above-mentioned failure of school pedagogy in its attempts to "educate the will."

Now as concerns the will itself, and the so-called "education of the will" or character-building (let us say, more accurately, with regard to the attainment of moral virtues and spiritual freedom), the specific task of school education amounts essentially to the two following points: first, the teacher must be solidly instructed in and deeply aware of the psychology of the child, less in order to form the latter's will and feelings than in order to avoid deforming or wounding them by pedagogical blunders to which unfortunately adults seem naturally inclined (here all of the modern psychological research may afford great help). Second, school and school life have to do, in an especially important manner, with what I would suggest calling "premoral" training, a point which deals not with morality strictly speaking, but with the preparation and first tilling of the soil thereof.* Yet the main duty in the educational spheres of the school as well as of the state is not to shape the will and directly to develop moral virtues in the youth, but to enlighten and strengthen reason; so it is that an indirect influence is exerted on the will, by a sound equipment of knowledge and a sound development of the powers of thinking.

Thus the paradox of which I have spoken at such length comes to a solution: what is most important in the upbringing of man, that is, the uprightness of the will and the

* The system of city schools as known in this country and tried here and there in Europe has proved particularly fruitful for such premoral training.

attainment of spiritual freedom, as well as the achievement of a sound relationship with society, is truly the main objective of education in its broadest sense. Concerning *direct* action on the will and the shaping of character, this objective chiefly depends on educational spheres other than school and college education—not to speak of the role which the extra-educational sphere plays in this matter. On the contrary, concerning *indirect* action on the will and the character, school and college education provides a basis and necessary preparation for the main objective in question by concentrating on knowledge and the intellect, not on the will and direct moral training, and by keeping sight, above all, of the development and uprightness of speculative and practical reason. School and college education has indeed its own world, which essentially consists of the dignity and achievements of knowledge and the intellect, that is, of the human being's root faculty. And of this world itself that knowledge which is wisdom is the ultimate goal.

II

THE DYNAMICS OF EDUCATION

IN the present chapter I shall consider the instrumentalities and dynamics of education. The main points to be examined will be: first, the dynamic factors or agents at work in education, which are the inner vitality of the student's mind and the activity of the teacher; second, the basic dispositions to be fostered in the pupil; third, the fundamental norms of education for the teacher.

1. THE DYNAMIC FACTORS

The Pupil's Mind and the Art of the Teacher

In order to discuss the dynamic factors in education, we must naturally reckon first with the Platonic conception: that all learning is in the learner, not in the teacher. Every reader of the *Phaedo* recalls that according to Plato knowledge preëxists from the very start in human souls, which before descending into the body have contemplated the eternal Ideas; but when these souls are bound to a body, they are prevented from freely considering those truths of which they already possess knowledge. The student, in this way, does not acquire knowledge from the teacher, who has no real causal influence and who is at best only an occasional agent: the teacher only awakens the attention of the student to those things which he already knows, so that to learn is nothing else than to remember.

There are great truths in these exaggerated views of Plato. And one cannot but wonder at the nobility and delicacy of his Socratic way of teaching which so ennobles the one who is taught—surely—since it deals with him as with an angel, asleep indeed, but nevertheless an angel. These educational views have been taken up afresh by many modern educators, though from quite different philosophical standpoints. In reality, however, things are not as Plato saw them who, after all, when treating of education from the political point of view in his *Laws* was to overemphasize so surprisingly the authoritative aspect of education. The teacher does possess a knowledge which the student does not have. He actually communicates knowledge to the student whose soul has *not* previously contemplated the divine Ideas before being united to his body; and whose intellect, before being fecundated by sense-perception and sense-experience, is but a *tabula rasa*, as Aristotle put it.

Yet what is the kind of causality or dynamic action exerted by the teacher? Teaching is an art; the teacher is an artist. Is the teacher, then, like a sculptor, a powerful Michelangelo who belabors the marble or despotically imposes the form he has conceived on the passive clay? Such a conception was not infrequent in the education of old. It is a coarse and disastrous conception, contrary to the nature of things. For if the one who is being taught is not an angel, neither is he inanimate clay.

It is rather with the art of medicine that the art of education must be compared. Medicine deals with a living being that possesses inner vitality and the internal principle of health. The doctor exerts real causality in healing a sick man, yes, but in a very particular manner: by imitating the ways of nature herself in her operations, and by helping nature, by providing appropriate diet and remedies that nature herself uses, according to her own dynamism, toward a biological equilibrium. In other words, medicine is *ars cooperativa naturae*, an art of ministering, an art subservient to nature. And so is education. The implications of this are far-reaching indeed.

Ready-made knowledge does not, as Plato believed, exist

in human souls. But the vital and active principle of knowledge does exist in each of us. The inner seeing power of intelligence, which naturally and from the very start perceives through sense-experience the primary notions on which all knowledge depends, is thereby able to proceed from what it already knows to what it does not yet know. An example of this is a Pascal discovering without any teacher and by virtue of his own ingenuity the first thirty-two propositions of the first book of Euclid. This inner vital principle the teacher must respect above all; his art consists in imitating the ways of the intellectual nature in its own operations. Thus the teacher has to offer to the mind either examples from experience or particular statements which the pupil is able to judge by virtue of what he already knows and from which he will go on to discover broader horizons. The teacher has further to comfort the mind of the pupil by putting before his eyes the logical connections between ideas which the analytical or deductive power of the pupil's mind is perhaps not strong enough to establish by itself.

All this boils down to the fact that the mind's natural activity on the part of the learner and the intellectual guidance on the part of the teacher are both dynamic factors in education, but that the principal agent in education, the primary dynamic factor or propelling force, is the internal vital principle in the one to be educated; the educator or teacher is only the secondary—though a genuinely effective—dynamic factor and a ministerial agent.

Education by the Rod and Progressive Education

Here, we teachers and professors may sometimes find consolation for our failures—we can think of them as due to the defect of the principal agent, the inner principle within the student, and not to our own deficiencies. And such an excuse is often valid. Yet quite apart from this kind of solace to teachers, the very simple considerations which I have just laid down in paraphrasing Thomas Aquinas, are, to my mind, of great import to the philosophy of education. I think that they illuminate the whole conflict between the old form of education by the rod and progressive education, which centers upon and stresses the freedom and the inner natural vitality of the child.

Education by the rod is positively bad education. If from a love of paradox I were to say something on its behalf, I should only observe that it has been able, actually, to produce some strong personalities, because it is difficult to kill the internal principle of spontaneity in living beings, and because this principle occasionally develops more powerfully when it reacts and sometimes revolts against constraint, fear, and punishment than when everything is made easy, lenient, and psychotechnically compliant to it. Strangely enough, we may wonder whether an education which yields itself entirely to the sovereignty of the child, and which suppresses any obstacle to be overcome, does not result in making students both indifferent and too docile, too passively permeable to anything the teacher is saying. However that may be, it is still true that birch and taws are bad educational measures, and that any education which considers the teacher as the principal agent perverts the very nature of the educational task.

The actual merit of modern conceptions in education since Pestalozzi, Rousseau, and Kant, has been the rediscovery of the fundamental truth that the principal agent and dynamic factor is not the art of the teacher but the inner principle of activity, the inner dynamism of nature and of the mind. If there were time we could insist, in this connection, that the search for new methods and inspiration, as emphasized by progressive education and what is called in Europe the "active school," should be valued, developed, and expanded—on condition that progressive education gives up its out-of-date rationalistic prejudices and utopian philosophy of life and does not forget that the teacher, too, is a real cause and agent—though only co-öperating with nature—a real giver whose own dynamism, moral authority, and positive guidance are indispensable. If this complementary aspect is forgotten, the finest endeavors which arise from the mere cult of the freedom of the child will be washed away in the sands.

The freedom of the child is not the spontaneity of animal nature, moving right from the start along the fixed determinate paths of instinct (at least we usually think of animal instinct in this form, which is really too simplified, for animal instinct has a first period of progressive fixation). The freedom of the child is the spontaneity of a human and rational nature, and this largely *undetermined* spontaneity has its inner principle of final determination only in reason, which is not yet developed in the child.

The plastic and suggestible freedom of the child is harmed and led astray if it is not helped and guided. An education which consisted in making the child responsible for acquiring information about that of which he does not know he is ignorant, an education which only contemplated a blossoming forth of the child's instincts, and which rendered the teacher a tractable and useless attendant, is but a bankruptcy of education and of the responsibility of adults toward the youth. The right of the child to be educated requires that the educator shall have moral authority over him, and this authority is nothing else than the duty of the adult to the freedom of the youth.

The True and the False Freeing of Personality

It is possible to get a more profound view of the matter if one remembers the distinction between "personality" and "individuality" that we stated in our first chapter. Here we are confronted with the crucial problem of the education of man, in the broadest sense of this word. Let me re-call that the distinction of which I am speaking is a meta-physical distinction which must be carefully understood, and which considers two different aspects of a same whole, of that same human being whom ordinary language calls equally an individual and a person.

The same man in his entirety is an individual and a per-son: he is a person by reason of the spiritual subsistence of his soul, and he is an individual by reason of that principle of nonspecific diversity which is matter, and which makes the components of a same species different from each other. My individuality and my personality, thus defined, are two aspects of my whole substantial being, to which correspond two different poles of attraction for my inner and moral development. I may develop along the lines of personality, that is, toward the mastery and independence of my spirit-ual self. Or I may develop along the lines of individuality, that is, toward the letting loose of the tendencies which are present in me by virtue of matter and heredity.

Such being the case, certain educators confuse person-ality with individuality, and mistake the display of sheer individuality for the development of personality. Per-sonality means interiority to oneself; this internal selfhood grows in proportion as the life of reason and freedom dom-inates over the life of instinct and sensual desire—which implies self-sacrifice, striving toward self-perfection and love. But individuality, in the strict Aristotelian sense in which I am using this word, individuality means the mate-rial ego, the displaying of which consists in giving a free, hand to the irrational trends of this ego. Thus, while be-coming the center of everything, the ego is in reality scat-tered among cheap desires or overwhelming passions, and finally submitted to the determinism of matter.

I have insisted that education must center on the devel-opment and liberation of the individual person. What I am criticizing is that false form of appreciation of the individual person which, while looking at individuality instead of personality, reduces the education and progress of man to the mere freeing of the material ego. Such educators mistakenly believe they are providing man with the freedom of expansion and autonomy to which personality aspires while at the same time they deny the value of all discipline and asceticism, as well as the necessity of striving toward self-perfection. As a result, instead of fulfilling himself, man disperses himself and disintegrates.

Other educators, contrariwise, misconstrue the distinction between personality and individuality as a separation. They think that we bear in ourselves two separate beings, that of the individual and that of the person. Such partisans of the rod advocate "Death to the individual! And long live the person!" Unfortunately, when you kill the individual you also kill the person. This *despotic* conception of the education and progress of man is no better than the *anarchical* one. The ideal of the despotic conception is first to take out our heart, with anesthetics if possible, and next to replace it by some perfect organ standardized according to the rules of what everyone ought to be. The first operation may perhaps succeed, the second one is more difficult. Instead of a genuine human personality, sealed with the mysterious face of its Creator, there appears a mask, that of the conventional man or that of the rubber-stamped conscience, "incorporated."

If it is true that the internal principle, that is to say, nature—and grace too, for man is not a merely natural being—is what matters most in education, it follows that the entire art consists in inspiring, schooling and pruning, teaching and enlightening, so that in the intimacy of man's activities the weight of the egoistic tendencies diminishes, and the weight of the aspirations proper to personality and its spiritual generosity increases.

It should be added that the very term "self-perfection," which I used a while ago, needs to be properly understood. Man's perfection consists of the perfection of love, and so is less the perfection of his "self" than the perfection of his love, where the very self is in some measure lost sight of. And to advance in this self-perfection is not to copy an ideal. It is to let yourself be led by Another where you did not want to go, and to let Divine Love Who calls each being by his own name mold you and make of you a person, a true original, not a copy.

2. THE FUNDAMENTAL DISPOSITIONS TO BE FOSTERED

We have had a view of the being who is to be formed into a true human person, perfecting himself by knowledge and by love, and capable of giving himself; and we have seen that to achieve rationality and freedom this being must have knowledge taught and discipline, and these require the office of the teacher. I now come to the second general topic, the basic dispositions of human nature.

If the nature and spirit of the child are the principal agent in education, then, obviously, the fundamental dispositions to be fostered in this principal agent are the very basis of the task of education. They are rooted in nature but they may be warped, and they need to be carefully cultivated. Without pretending to a complete enumeration, I should say that the fundamental dispositions are the five following ones:

With Regard to Truth and Justice

First, the love of truth, which is the primary tendency of any intellectual nature. (That children tell lies is obvious, yet most often the lies of children are not lies but only a spontaneous mythology of the imagination. Besides I am not thinking now of a love of telling the truth but of the love for knowing the truth).

Second, the love of good and justice, and even the love of heroic feats, and this too is natural to the children of man.

With Regard to Existence

Third, that disposition which might be called simplicity and openness with regard to existence. A disposition which is natural, though often thwarted by egotism or pride or unhappy experiences, and which is so elemental that we cannot easily express it in terms of psychology. For nothing is more basic and elemental than that to which it refers, that is, existence. I would describe this disposition as the attitude of a being who *exists* gladly, is unashamed of existing, stands upright in existence, and for whom to be and to accept the natural limitations of existence are matters of equally simple assent. Trees and animals are like this, though only in a physical way. In man this has to pass over and be drawn into the sphere of psychic life. We can interpret in this way the saying of Emerson: "Be first a good animal."* Such a disposition is still far from the human virtues of magnanimity and humility, but it constitutes

---

* Yet a child of man must "be first a good animal" in exhibiting the features of the root generosity, the spontaneous intelligence and the *gentleness* proper to humanity. Thus the simplicity and openness which I mean are the opposite of that egotistic and obtrusive self-consciousness which gets rid of shame and anguish only to substitute hardness and insensitiveness, and which does not *accept* existence but selfishly and greedily *monopolizes* it. Such self-consciousness easily turns into a self-protecting injustice, and forms its own "subjective" truths that suit the ego better than the "real" truth. When the age of reflection arrives, *simplicity with regard to existence* will normally become the basis of an intellectual awakening to the problem of existence; but *callous self-consciousness* will close the mind to any metaphysical anxiety, and develop into that metallic imperviousness which characterizes so many men and women of our day. If the latter disposition were mistaken for the former, the result would be such that we would even find attractive the poor little wretch, the neurotic, the child with a damaged ego, who was forced at least to wonder why he was living, and who thus developed enough spiritual disquietude to concern himself with the problems and pains of philosophy and religion, poetry, art, or love.

their natural soil; and it is so deeply and elementarily vital that the wounds it happens to undergo in many children, often very early, from family life and social life—spoken of today as an inferiority complex with its manifold morbid "compensations"—are especially grievous and difficult to cure. "Fear and trembling," undoubtedly, are part of the great experiences of the human soul, when it has become mature and enters the mysterious avenues of the spirit, but they are bad beginnings in education. At the dawn of our history the misfortune of mankind was that it was bound to begin its education under their shadow.

With Regard to Work

The fourth fundamental disposition concerns the sense of a job well done, for next to the attitude toward existence there is nothing more basic in man's psychic life than the attitude toward work. I do not mean by this the habit of being hard working. I am aware that laziness, as well as pride, is natural to us. Moreover laziness in children is often not real laziness but only an absorption of the mind with the workings of vegetative growth or psychophysical hardships. I am speaking of something deeper and more human, a respect for the job to be done, a feeling of faithfulness and responsibility regarding it. A lazy man, a poet if you will, may display, when he happens to work, the most passionate attachment to the inner requirements of his work. I am convinced that when this fundamental disposition, which is the first natural move toward self-discipline, this probity in regard to work is marred, an essential basis of human morality is lacking.

With Regard to the Others

The fifth fundamental disposition is the sense of coöperation, which is as natural in us, and as thwarted too, as the tendency to social and political life.

3. THE FUNDAMENTAL NORMS OF EDUCATION

The First Rule

Now I arrive at my third section: the fundamental rules of education for the teacher or the ministerial agent. Assuredly, the primary rule is to foster those fundamental dispositions which enable the principal agent to grow in the life of the mind. It is clear, in this connection, that the task of the teacher is above all one of liberation. To liberate the good energies is the best way of repressing the bad ones, though repression is also needed, but only as a secondary means, as dealing particularly with that part of animal training in human education of which I spoke in my first chapter, and even so it is useful only on condition that the repression of bad tendencies will always be bound up with enlightenment and encouragement. Encouragement is as fundamentally necessary as humiliation is harmful. A mere prohibition of evil-doing is less efficacious than illumination about the good that this evil-doing will spoil. The real art is to make the child heedful of his own resources and potentialities for the beauty of well-doing.

The Second Rule

The second fundamental norm is to center attention on the inner depths of personality and its preconscious spiritual dynamism, in other words, to lay stress on inwardness and the internalization of the educational influence.

We have good reason to believe that a particular weakness in our educational methods comes from the rationalistic approach which developed for two centuries, and from the Cartesian psychology of clear and distinct ideas which impaired traditional as well as progressive education, and which grew poorer and more unreal in proportion as it was associated with the sheer empiricist mentality that prevailed in modern philosophy. The pressure on the surface level of the mind of ready-made formulas of knowledge, as elaborated for the socialized intellectual life of adults, and only made cheaper and more rudimentary for the use of children, and the pressure on the surface level of the will, either of compulsory discipline or of extraneous incentives motivated by self-interest and competition, have left the internal world of the child's soul either dormant or bewildered and rebellious.

An English writer, Gerald Heard,* who has been, I believe, the spiritual instructor of Aldous Huxley, has expressed the opinion that after what he calls the "eotechnic" stage of classical education and the present "paleotechnic" stage of progressive education, a "neotechnic" stage is now to come, which will be concerned with the subconscious powers and activity of the child. This may be true, and it may be real progress, on condition, however, that this new stage also progresses beyond the general philosophy of Gerald Heard and its contempt for the intellect and its superstitious trust in techniques.

At this point it is all important to make clear that the word subconscious or unconscious covers two thoroughly different, though intermingled, fields. One is that field explored with special eagerness by the Freudian School, the field of the instincts, latent images, affective impulses, and sensual tendencies which should be called the unconscious of the irrational in man. The other, missed by the Freudians, is the field of the root life of those spiritual powers, the intellect and the will, the fathomless abyss of personal freedom and of the personal thirst and striving for knowing and seeing, grasping and expressing—I should call this the preconscious of the spirit in man. For reason does not consist only of its conscious logical tools and manifes-

* Gerald Heard, *A Quaker Mutation*, Pendle Hill Pamphlet No. 7 1940.

tations nor does the will consist only of its deliberate conscious determinations. Far beneath the apparent surface of
explicit concepts and judgments, of words and expressed
resolutions or movements of the will, are the sources of
knowledge and poetry, of love and truly human desires,
hidden in the spiritual darkness of the intimate vitality of
the soul. Before being formed and expressed in concepts
and judgments, intellectual knowledge is at first a beginning of insight, still unformulated, which proceeds from
the impact of the illuminating activity of the intellect on
the world of images and emotions and which is but a humble
and trembling movement, yet invaluable, toward an intelligible content to be grasped. Parenthetically, it is with
reference to this preconscious spiritual dynamism of
human personality that keeping personal contact with the
pupil is of such great import, not only as a better technique
for making study more attractive and stimulating, but
above all to give to that mysterious identity of the child's
soul, which is unknown to himself, and which no techniques
can reach, the comforting assurance of being in some way
recognized by a human personal gaze, inexpressible either
in concepts or words.

Both the irrational subconscious and the preconscious of
the spirit involve a deep internal dynamism. These depths
of the human being are moreover in vital connection with
one another and may interfere or intermingle in many
ways. Yet they are thoroughly different in their very nature. When man seeking for his own inner universe takes
the wrong road, he enters the internal world of the irrational unconscious, while believing he enters the internal
world of the spirit, and he thus finds himself wandering in a
false kind of self-interiority, where wildness and automa-
tism mimic freedom. Such has been the adventure, I note
in passing, of some pseudo-mystics or illuminati, and more
recently, of the surrealist poets, some of them true poets

but led astray by their system. In reality that to which we are called by our genuinely human aspirations is to free and purify the spiritual unconscious from the irrational one, and to find our sources of life and liberty and peace in this purified preconsciousness of the spirit.

The Freeing of the Intuitive Power

Of course education has a great deal to do with the irrational subconscious dynamism of the child's psyche. But, particularly in the case of school and college education, it is with the preconscious or the subconscious of the spirit that education is mainly concerned.

I hate the idea of a training of the subconscious—of the subconscious of the irrational—by means of I know not what yogism or techniques of suggestion. If the "neotechnic" age of education would proceed in this way, and deliver the child's soul over to be rifled by teachers transformed into modelers of the subconscious, it would be a bad omen for freedom and reason. But if we consider the other subconscious, the preconscious of the spirit, here we see that important and helpful changes might take place in our educational methods. Here it is not a question of techniques, nor of a training of the subconscious. It is rather a question of liberating the vital preconscious sources of the spirit's activity. Using Bergsonian language, I would say that in the education of the mind the emphasis should be shifted from that which is *pressure* (which, of course, remains somewhat necessary, but secondary) to that which awakens and frees the *aspirations* of spiritual nature in us. Thus creative imagination, and the very life of the intellect, would not be sacrificed to cramming memorization or to conventional rules of skill in making use of concepts or words, or to the honest and conscientious but mechanical and hopeless cultivation of overspecialized fields of learning.

With regard to the development of the human mind, neither the richest material facilities nor the richest equipment in methods, information, and erudition are the main point. The great thing is the awakening of the inner resources and creativity. The cult of technical means considered as improving the mind and producing science by their own virtue must give way to respect for the spirit and dawning intellect of man! Education thus calls for an intellectual sympathy and intuition on the part of the teacher, concern for the questions and difficulties with which the mind of the youth may be entangled without being able to give expression to them, a readiness to be at hand with the lessons of logic and reasoning that invite to action the unexercised reason of the youth. No tricks can do that, no set of techniques, but only personal attention to the inner blossoming of the rational nature and then confronting that budding reason with a system of rational knowledge.

What matters most in the life of reason is intellectual insight or intuition. There is no training or learning for that. Yet if the teacher keeps in view above all the inner center of vitality at work in the preconscious depths of the life of the intelligence, he may center the acquisition of knowledge and solid formation of the mind on the freeing of the child's and the youth's intuitive power. By what means? By moving forward along the paths of spontaneous interest and natural curiosity, by grounding the exercise of memory in intelligence, and primarily by giving courage, by listening a great deal, and by causing the youth to trust and give expression to those spontaneous poetic or noetic impulses of his own which seem to him fragile and bizarre, because they are not assured by any social sanction—and in fact any awkward gesture or rebuff or untimely advice on the part of the teacher can crush such timid sproutings and push them back into the shell of the unconscious.

I should like, moreover, to suggest that, in order to set free creative and perceptive intellectual intuition, the path through which it is naturally awakened, the path of sense-perception and sense-experience and imagination, should be respected and followed as far as possible by the teacher. Above all the liberation of which we are speaking depends essentially on the free adhesion of the mind to the objective reality to be seen. Let us never deceive or rebuke the thirst for seeing in youth's intelligence! The freeing of the intuitive power is achieved in the soul through the object grasped, the intelligible grasping toward which this power naturally tends. The germ of insight starts within a preconscious intellectual cloud, arising from experience, imagination, and a kind of spiritual feeling, but it is from the outset a tending toward an object to be grasped. And to the extent that this tendency is set free and the intellect becomes accustomed to grasping, seeing, expressing the objects toward which it tends, to that very extent its intuitive power is liberated and strengthened. Before giving a youth the rules of good style, let us tell him first never to write anything which does not seem to him really beautiful, whatever the result may be. In the first approach to mathematics, physics, or philosophy, let us see to it that the student actually grasps each step of the simplest mathematical demonstration, however slow this may be—that he actually understands in the laboratory how logically the statement of the physicist emerges from the experiment—that he becomes intensely involved, through the very anxiety of his mind, in the first great philosophical problems, and after that, that he really sees the solution. In asking a youth to read a book, let us get him to undertake a real spiritual adventure and meet and struggle with the internal world of a given man, instead of glancing over a collection of bits of thought and dead opinions, looked upon from without and with sheer indifference, according to the horrible custom of so many victims of what they call "being informed." Perhaps with such methods the curriculum will lose a little in scope, which will be all to the good.*

Finally the very mood of the teaching is here of crucial import. If a teacher himself is concerned with discerning and seeing, with getting vision, rather than with collecting facts and opinions, and if he handles his burden of knowledge so as to see through it into the reality of things, then in the mind of the student the power of intuition will be awakened and strengthened unawares, by the very intuitivity traversing such teaching.

The Third Rule

I come now to the third fundamental rule, which I shall try to express as follows: the whole work of education and teaching must tend to unify, not to spread out; it must strive to foster internal unity in man.

This means that from the very start, and, as far as possible, all through the years of youth, hands and mind should be at work together. This point has been made particularly clear by modern pedagogy as regards childhood. It is also valid for youth. The importance of manual work accompanying the education of the mind during the high school and college training is more and more recognized. There is no place closer to man than a workshop, and the intelligence of a man is not only in his head, but in his fingers too. Not only does manual work further psychological equilibrium, but it also furthers ingenuity and accuracy of the mind, and is the prime basis of artistic activity. Occasionally—and the state of the world during and after the present war will perhaps require imperatively such a task

---

* With such methods, in any case, we would give up that peculiar procedure in examinations, which consists in asking the student to check as true or false a certain number of ready-made sentences, astutely prepared by the teachers, and which seems calculated to kill any personal effort of thought and expression.

—youth might coöperate in many kinds of labor, harvesting, for instance, needed for the common welfare. But as a rule, and from the educational point of view, it is craftsman's labor—and also, for the sake of our mechanical age, mechanical and constructive dexterity—that should constitute the manual training of which I am speaking. I should like to add that this emphasis on manual work in education seems to me to correspond to a general characteristic of the world of tomorrow, where the dignity of work will probably be more clearly recognized, and the social cleavage between *homo faber* and *homo sapiens* done away with.

A second implication of the rule we are discussing is that education and teaching must start with experience, but in order to complete themselves with reason. This is obvious and needs no elucidation, save perhaps that special stress should be laid upon the second part of the statement, in an age where an empiricist philosophy often makes capital out of experience, and the highest functions of reason and the insights of abstract thought are disregarded. To be sure, sense-experience is the very origin of all our knowledge, and education must follow the course of nature. Modern methods are perfectly aware of that, especially with children. The point, however, is to disengage from experience the rational and necessary connections with which that experience is pregnant, and which become visible only by means of abstraction and universal concepts, and in the light of the intuitive first principles of reason. Thus knowledge and science arise from experience. Neither those empiricists who despise abstract reason, logic, and the conceptual insights of intelligence, nor those rationalists who ignore experience, are integrated minds. Education must inspire eagerness both for experience and for reason, teach reason to base itself on facts and experience to realize itself in rational knowledge, grounded on principles, looking at the *raisons d'être*, causes and ends, and grasping reality in terms of how and why.

Spiritual Unity and Wisdom

Yet what the present rule means basically is that education and teaching should never lose sight of the organic unity of the task to be performed, and of the essential need and aspiration of the mind to be freed in unity. If a man does not overcome the inner multiplicity of his drives and especially of the diverse currents of knowledge and belief and the diverse vital energies at play in his mind, he will always remain more a slave than a free man. Tears, sweat, and blood are needed for this all too difficult task of unifying our internal world. The school should help us in this effort, and not impair it and make it hopeless. The dispersion and atomization of human life are in our day the great distress of the adult world. Instead of opening itself more and more to this devastating dispersion, the school system at least should prepare us to surmount it, and provide our youth with a more fortunate world of its own, fitted to our spiritual demand and centered on unity.*

Undoubtedly the tremendous multiplicity of the fields of knowledge, due to the very progress of modern science, makes the work of unification more difficult than ever. Yet a great symphony can and must have internal unity as well as a piece of chamber music. What is wanted here is nothing less than inspiration and vision.

In order to establish an organic and architectonic order-

---

* In his essay, *The Universities Look for Unity* (Pantheon Books, New York, 1943), which develops the chapter dedicated to "Education" in his remarkable volume *The United States and Civilization,* Professor Nef strongly emphasizes this need for unity and offers practical reforms of great interest. For lack of space I can only allude to these inspiring suggestions. It is to be hoped that they will be thoroughly examined and discussed by university men aware of present-day problems. See below, page 81.

ing of teaching, the prerequisite background is a sound philosophy of knowledge and of the degrees of knowledge, but the inspiring motive force is the vision embracing the whole practical dynamism of teaching. And toward what can such a vision be directed, except the very goal of this dynamism? And what is this very goal but wisdom? That knowledge we call wisdom, which penetrates and embraces things with the deepest, most universal, and most united insights. Such a knowledge, which lives not only by supreme science, but also by human and spiritual experience, is over and above any field of specialization, for it has to do with realities which permeate each and every being and with aspirations which call to the very nature and freedom of man. It is in itself the highest value for the human mind. Education and teaching can only achieve their internal unity if the manifold parts of their whole work are organized and quickened by a vision of wisdom as the supreme goal, so as progressively to make youth capable of sharing to some degree in the intellectual and moral fruits of wisdom.

The purpose of elementary and higher education is not to make of the youth a truly wise man, but to equip his mind with an ordered knowledge which will enable him to advance toward wisdom in his manhood. Its specific aim is to provide him with the foundations of real wisdom, and with a universal and articulate comprehension of human achievements in science and culture, before he enters upon the definite and limited tasks of adult life in the civil community, and even while he is preparing himself for these tasks through a specialized scientific, technical, or vocational training.

Such a universal and articulate comprehension of human achievements in science and culture, such a "music" of the wit, as Plato put it, takes shape in profoundly different ways on the several levels of education. In each of the great educational divisions which correspond to the main periods of the youth's life, from the years of childhood to the years of university and graduate study, we have to face a mental world of comprehensive universality which has only a proportional similarity with the mental worlds of other levels. The universality adapted to the young readers of fairy tales and *Alice in Wonderland* is of quite another nature than that fitted to the students reading Kant or Spinoza. Yet each educational stage deals with a comprehensive universality of its own, approaching little by little that of maturity, and at each stage education should be guided by the vision of the appropriate mental world of comprehensive or "symphonic" universality. And this vision should be communicated in some way to the ones who are taught, in order to make them realize the vital interest of their task and to give them inspiration and energy. What are known in this country as "orientation courses" are stimulating beginnings and attempts in this direction, although they are still, it seems to me, in the nature of a compensation and palliative rather than a token of a general recasting of the educational scheme.

The Fourth Rule

Finally there is a fourth fundamental rule, which demands that teaching liberate intelligence instead of burdening it, in other words, that teaching result in the freeing of the mind through the mastery of reason over the things learned.

Pascal's father, who was the instructor of his son, used to emphasize a maxim which seems to me very significant in this connection. Gilberte Pascal, the sister, writes: "It was a chief maxim of his in the education of his son that the child must always be kept *above his work* (*au-dessus de son ouvrage*)," or master of his work. "It was for this reason," she goes on to say, "that he refused to begin to teach him

Latin before the child was twelve, so that he might do so more easily," and this was a great innovation in the French education of that time. He also prevented his son from learning mathematics as long as possible—he concealed from him any book of mathematics and refrained from discussing mathematical questions with his friends in the presence of the youth—for "he knew mathematics to be a science which fills up and satisfies the mind," and easily gains too strong a domination over it—he was suspicious of Platonism. Mathematics was to take a fine revenge on him.

Other great maxims could be recalled in this connection. The rule of Thomas Aquinas, in his own studies, was "never to leave behind him any difficulty unsolved." "Always make sure," he warned students, "that you actually understand what you read or listen to," and "avoid speechifying on anything whatsoever." He also warned teachers —this advice was already necessary for the educators of his time—"never to dig," in front of the steps of the student, "never to dig a ditch that you fail to fill up." He knew that to raise clever doubts, to prefer searching to finding, and perpetually to pose problems without ever solving them are the great enemies of education.

To summarize: What is learned should never be passively or mechanically received, as dead information which weighs down and dulls the mind. It must rather be actively transformed by understanding into the very life of the mind, and thus strengthen the latter, as wood thrown into fire and transformed into flame makes the fire stronger. But a big mass of damp wood thrown into the fire only puts it out. Reason which receives knowledge in a servile manner does not really know and is only depressed by a knowledge which is not its own but that of others. On the contrary, reason which receives knowledge by assimilating it vitally, that is, in a free and liberating manner, really knows, and is exalted in its very activity by this knowledge which henceforth is its own. Then it is that reason really masters the things learned.

Knowledge and Training

We are confronted here with the notion of mental training which at the time of John Locke* was already emphasized by the adversaries of the liberal arts, and with the opposition so frequently aired between knowledge-value and training-value. Does the liberation of the mind mean that what essentially matters is not the possession of knowledge but only the development of the strength, skill, and accuracy of man's mental powers, whatever the thing to be learned may be? This question is of tremendous significance, and the wrong answer has probably gone a long way to water down contemporary education.

The observation has been made that, according to modern psychology, it is very questionable whether exercising a faculty upon a particular field of material improves this faculty in regard to any other kind of material to which it can be applied. Herbert Spencer long ago pointed out that if we give our pupils the knowledge which is "of most worth," as he put it, it is incredible that the pursuit of the best kind of knowledge should not also afford the best mental discipline.† From quite another philosophical point of view than that of Spencer, I think his statement to be a golden one. The knowledge which is "of most worth"—I don't mean which has the most practical value, I mean which makes the mind penetrate into those things which are the richest in truth and intelligibility—such knowledge affords by itself the best mental training, for it is by grasping the object and having itself seized and vitalized by truth that the human mind gains both its

---

* Cf. Cardinal John Henry Newman, *On the Scope and Nature of University Education,* Discourse VI, pp. 151–153. Everyman's Library.
† Cf. Sir T. Percy Nunn, "Education," *Encyclopaedia Britannica.*

strength and its freedom. It is not by the gymnastics of its faculties, it is by truth that it is set free, when truth is really known, that is, vitally assimilated by the insatiable activity which is rooted in the depths of self. The opposition between knowledge-value and training-value comes from an ignorance of what knowledge is, from the assumption that knowledge is a cramming of materials into a bag, and not the most vital action by means of which things are spiritualized in order to become one with the spirit. In the knowledge which is "of most worth," notably in the liberal arts, to give the upper hand to mental training, or to the mere dialectical disquisition of how great works are made or how great thoughts go on, to give such training the upper hand over beauty to be delighted in* or the truth

---

* I purposely stress this element of *delight* in the grasping of beauty, for delight pertains to the very essence of beauty: *ad rationem pulchri pertinet, quod in ejus aspectu seu cognitione quietetur appetitus.* St. Thomas Aquinas, *Sum. theol.,* I-II, 27, 1, ad 3. Unless we delight in and are moved by a work of art, we may thoroughly discuss and analyze it but we shall never understand it. Am I preaching here that "communication of ecstasy" of which Dr. Robert Hutchins makes such fun, and which he describes as the "thrill" that a work of art "sends down your spine"? *Education for Freedom,* p. 55. Please God that the teacher in fine arts may "communicate ecstasy" to his pupils! Yet in reality the delight transmitted by beauty thrills not only the senses but also, and first of all, the intuitiveness of intelligence and spirit. Neither the "historical" approach, freeing us from the consideration of the works themselves, nor any irrational and merely sensuous "communication of ecstasy" is an appropriate method. The good method requires first the intuitive delight, both emotional and intellectual, in the work's beauty, second, the rational disquisition of the very causes of this delight and of the intelligible regulations by which the work has been internally and vitally ruled and structured. It is necessary to make clear for the understanding of the pupil the inner logic of a Mozart sonata, read and discussed from the score. But it is first necessary for the pupil to hear the sonata, and be delighted in it, and love it with his ears and with his heart. Man's senses are not that impure element which Kant's puritanism abhorred. They are not unworthy of reason, they naturally serve reason and convey its food to it: *Visus et auditus rationi deservientes. Sum. theol.,* I-II, 27, 1, ad 3. "The sense," St. Thomas says, "delights in things duly proportioned, as in things similar to itself, for the sense itself is a

to be apprehended and assented to, would be to turn upside down the natural and vital tendency of the mind and drift toward dilettantism—and a dilettante has certainly a weak and not a well-trained mind.

There are people who think that it is wonderful to have a mind that is quick, clever, ready to see pros and cons, eager to discuss, and to discuss anything, and who believe that such a mind is that to which university education must give scope—regardless of *what* is thought about, *what* is discussed, and *how important* the matter is. These people are unaware that if they succeeded in making such a conception prevail, they would at best transform universities into schools of sophistry. In fact, they would not even produce sophists, who have some force, but rather disarmed and talkative minds, that believe they are well informed but live by words and opinions. Such persons are afraid to face reality, especially when reality is intellectually difficult and stringent, deep or dire, and they replace the personal effort to grasp things as they are with a ceaseless comparison of opinions. Youth taught according to this pattern may furnish excellent specialists in the field of technique and the sciences of matter, precisely because in this field such educational patterns cannot be applied. For the rest, in all that has regard to the understanding of man and culture and the highest and the most urgent human problems, not only do they develop a helpless nominalistic timidity, but they are absolutely lost in the midst of matters of knowledge and discussion the inner value and the respective importance of which they cannot and do not want to discern and recognize. For if we begin by denying that any subject matter is in itself and by reason of truth more important than another, then we deny

kind of *reason* (or vital proportion), like every knowing power." *Sum. theol.*, I, 5, 4, ad 1.

in reality that any subject matter has any importance in itself, and everything vanishes into futility.

I suppose that the general influence of contemporary instrumentalist philosophy shares some responsibility for the educational conception which I am criticizing, though the main incentive is rather to be found in the self-styled realism of the so-called practical man who scorns ideas and asks what is truth, with a patronizing indifference, not knowing that he is scorning the very source of human action, efficiency, and practicality.

In an address delivered in 1940 at Yale University, President Robert Hutchins, who purposely makes his voice sound unfriendly in order better to stimulate his friends, stated that "today the young American comprehends the intellectual tradition of which he is a part and in which he must live only by accident: for its scattered and disjointed fragments are strewn from one end of the campus to the other. Our university graduates have far more information and far less understanding than in the colonial period."* I am in no way entitled to express any opinion as to the accuracy or inaccuracy of Mr. Hutchins' judgment. But one statement I am sure he was right in making: "The crucial error," he also said, "is that of holding that nothing is any more important than anything else, that there can be no order of goods and no order in the intellectual realm. There is nothing central and nothing peripheral, nothing primary and nothing secondary, nothing basic and nothing superficial." In such conditions "the course of study goes to pieces because there is nothing to hold it together." We are facing there a result of the fact that too often contemporary education has deemed it suit-

* "The Higher Learning in America: 1940." Address to the Phi Beta Kappa delivered at Yale University. Part of this address forms the second chapter of *Education for Freedom*. My quotations refer to pages 25 and 26 of this volume.

able to substitute training-value for knowledge-value—in other words, mental gymnastics for truth, and being in fine fettle, for wisdom.

The Inner Structure of the Curriculum

Yet the opposition between knowledge-value and training-value may be understood in another way and help us to make useful discrimination in the field of teaching and school exercises. There are school subjects—those whose knowledge is "of most worth"—the main value of which is knowledge-value. And there are subjects—those whose knowledge is "of least worth"—the main value of which (I don't say the only value) is that of training. I should like to place the latter in the category of play—in broadening, of course, the sense of this word—and the former in the category of learning. Play has an essential part, though secondary, in school life; it possesses a value and worth of its own, being the activity of free expansion and a gleam of poetry in the very field of those energies which tend by nature toward utility. In the category of play thus broadly understood, I should like to see many things which are taught in elementary and secondary education—not only games, sports, and physical training, but first of all that handicraft work and dexterity in mechanics of which I spoke earlier, and, moreover, everything that the school can fancy to give training in, gardening, beekeeping, rustic lore, even cooking, jam-making, home economics, and so forth, and what is known as artistic training insofar as the "arts" involved are what is called in French *les arts d'agrément*, and in English, if I am not mistaken, "accomplishments." All of these things are dignified if they are dealt with as play activity, not with too much seriousness or too many frowns, but with some free and poetical cheerfulness. They lose educational meaning and make the school ever so slightly absurd if they are dealt with as an activity of learning, and put on the same level as genuine learning.

Above the category of play comes the category of learning, devoted to those matters whose main value is knowledge-value. Here too I think it would be best to trace a line of demarcation. In a first division we would place those matters the knowledge of which concerns the intellectual instruments and logical discipline required for the achievements of reason, as well as the treasure of factual and experiential information which must be gathered in memory. In a second division should be placed those matters the knowledge of which refers directly to the creative or perceptive intuition of the intellect and to that thirst for seeing of which we spoke previously.

In the first division I should like to place grammar, with a view to comparative grammar and philology, logic, and languages, on the other hand history, national history as well as the history of man and civilization and especially the history of the sciences, with connected subjects such as geography; all this I should call the field of the pre-liberal arts. And I should like to see the second division as the field of liberal arts, by recasting the old sevenfold listing of the Middle Ages according to a strictly educational outlook and to the modern progress of knowledge. Our *trivium* would concern the creative activity of the mind, and beauty to be perceived and delighted in. To begin with, it would comprise that *Eloquence* represented by Calliope, the first Muse and the mother of Orpheus, that is to say, the art of thought-expression or creative-expression which is the very art of making the mind actually able to set free and manifest its creative insight and making it really master of its power of expression—an art the neglect of which is so harmful to modern youth, who often lose their sense of the worthiness and accuracy of words, and become unable even to compose, when they enter upon

practical life, a clear and articulate report on commercial
or industrial matters. Then we would have, as the second
of the liberal arts, *Literature and Poetry*, and as the third
one, *Music and Fine Arts*.

Our *quadrivium* would concern the knowing and rational
activity, the intuitive and judicative activity of the mind
—truth to be perceived and assented to "according to
the worth of evidence." It would comprise first, *Mathematics*, second, *Physics and the Natural Sciences*, third,
Philosophy—I mean not only psychology, but also the
philosophy of nature, metaphysics, and the theory of
knowledge—and fourth *Ethics and Political and Social
Philosophy*, and connected studies.

This glimpse of the inner structure and organization of
the curriculum illustrates the principles of this chapter on
the dynamics of education, in the course of which we have
distinguished two dynamic factors—the natural activity of
the pupil's mind and the ministerial art of the teacher—
five basic dispositions in the pupil, and four fundamental
rules for the teacher. These rules have to do first with the
natural dispositions to be fostered, second, with the preconscious of the spirit to be kept sight of and the intuitive
power to be set free; third, with the vital unity to be maintained and a vision of wisdom to be preserved all along the
process of teaching; and fourth, with the liberation of the
mind through the mastery of reason over what is learned
and through the primacy of real knowledge over mere
training.

III

THE HUMANITIES AND LIBERAL EDUCATION

IN this third chapter I shall touch upon the three great stages of education: elementary education, the humanities, advanced studies. In reference to the second stage—the humanities—we shall have to discuss some problems concerning college and the curriculum; in reference to the third stage—advanced studies—I should like to outline the idea of a modern university, as the consummation of liberal education.

1. THE RUDIMENTS

The Spheres of Knowledge

As to the principal stages in education, let us note that there are three great periods in education. I should like to designate them as the rudiments (or elementary education), the humanities (comprising both secondary and college education), and advanced studies (comprising graduate schools and higher specialized learning). And these periods correspond not only to three natural chronological periods in the growth of the youth but also to three naturally distinct and qualitatively determinate spheres of psychological development, and, accordingly, of knowledge.

The physical structure of the child is not that of the adult, shortened and abridged. The child is not a dwarf man. Nor is the adolescent. And this is much truer and much more crucial as regards the psychological than the physical structure of the youth. In the realm of physical training, of psychophysical conditioning, of animal and experimental psychology, contemporary education has understood more and more perfectly that a child of man is not just a diminutive man. It has not yet understood this in the spiritual realm of knowing: because, indeed, it is not interested in the psychology of spiritual activities. How, therefore, could it do anything but ignore that realm? The error is twofold. First we have forgotten that science and knowledge are not a self-sufficient set of notions, existing for their own sakes, abstracted and separate from man. Science and knowledge don't exist in books, they do exist in minds, they are vital and internal energies and must develop therefore according to the inner spiritual structure of the mind in which they have their being.

Secondly, we act as if the task of education were to infuse into the child or the adolescent, only abridging and concentrating it, the very science or knowledge of the adult —that is to say, of the philologist, the historian, the grammarian, the scientist, etc., the most specialized experts. So we try to cram young people with a chaos of summarized adult notions which have been either condensed, dogmatized, and textbookishly cut up or else made so easy that they are reduced to the vanishing point. As a result, we run the risk of producing either an instructed, bewildered intellectual dwarf, or an ignorant intellectual dwarf playing at dolls with our science. In a recent essay Professor Douglas Bush recalls "the classic anecdote of the young woman who was asked if she could teach English history. 'Oh yes,' she replied brightly, 'I've had it twice, once in clay and once in sand.' " *

The knowledge to be given to youth *is not* the same

* Douglas Bush, *Science, Philosophy and Religion,* Second Symposium (New York, 1942), p. 325.

knowledge as that of adults, it is an intrinsically and basically different knowledge,* which is not knowledge in the state of science, such as that possessed by the mind of the adult, but the specific knowledge fitted to quicken and perfect the original world of thought of the child and the adolescent. Consequently I should like to emphasize that at each stage the knowledge must be of a sort fitted to the learners and conceived as reaching its perfection within their universe of thought during a distinct period of their development, instead of laying the foundations of a single sphere of knowledge which would grow in a continuous and uniform way until it became the science of the adult, where alone it would attain perfection.

The Child

The universe of a child is the universe of imagination— of an imagination which evolves little by little into reason. The knowledge which has to be given to the child is knowledge in a state of story, an imaginative grasp of the things and values of the world. The child's mentality may be compared in some ways with that of primitive man, and this mentality tends by itself toward magic, and whatever effort the teacher may make, his teaching always runs the risk of being caught and engulfed in a magic ocean. In his task of civilizing the child's mind, therefore, he must progressively tame the imagination to the rule of reason, whilst ever remembering that the proportionally tremendous work of the child's intellect, endeavoring to grasp the external

---

* This knowledge is basically different from adult knowledge with regard to the *manner of knowing* or the intrinsic structure and perspective of knowledge itself. If, on the contrary, it were a question of the subject matter or the world of realities to be learned, we should state, as Comenius did three centuries ago, that from the lowest grade in the school system to the topmost level of university instruction, the content or subject of study is the same. Cf. Alexander Meiklejohn, *Education between Two Worlds* (New York, 1942), p. 19.

world, is accomplished under the vital and perfectly normal rule of imagination.

I should like to add that beauty is the mental atmosphere and the inspiring power fitted to a child's education, and should be, so to speak, the continuous quickening and spiritualizing contrapuntal base of that education. Beauty makes intelligibility pass unawares through sense-awareness. It is by virtue of the allure of beautiful things and deeds and ideas that the child is to be led and awakened to intellectual and moral life.

On the other hand the vitality and intuitiveness of the spirit are quick in the young child and sometimes pierce the world of his imaginative thought with the purest and most surprising flashes, as if his spirit, being not yet both strengthened and organized by the exercise of reason, enjoyed a kind of bounding, temperamental, and lucid freedom. At the same time, however, the immature workings of instinct and the violence of nature make him capable of intense resentment, wickedness, and manifold perversion. This vitality of the spirit should be relied upon as an invaluable factor in the first stages of education. Even from a purely naturalistic point of view it is a pity to see the child's mysterious expectant gravity and his resources as regards spiritual life neglected or trampled upon by his elders, either from some positivist bias or because they think it is their duty, when they deal with children, to make themselves childish.

2. THE HUMANITIES

The Adolescent

The universe of the adolescent is a transition state on the way to the universe of man. Judgment and intellectual strength are developing but are not yet really acquired. Such a mobile and anxious universe evolves under the rule

of the natural impulses and tendencies of intelligence—an
intelligence which is not yet matured and strengthened by
those inner living energies, the sciences, arts, and wisdom,
but which is sharp and fresh, eager to pass judgment on
everything, and both trustful and exacting, and which
craves intuitive sight. The knowledge which has to develop
in the adolescent is knowledge appealing to the natural
powers and gifts of the mind, knowledge as tending toward all things by the natural instinct of intelligence. The
mental atmosphere for adolescence should be one of truth
to be embraced. Truth is the inspiring force needed in the
education of the youth—truth rather than erudition and
self-consciousness—all-pervading truth rather than the
objectively isolated truth at which each of the diverse
sciences aims. Here we are confronted with a natural and
instinctive impulse toward some all-embracing truth, which
must be shaped little by little to critical reflection, but
which I should like to compare primarily to the trend of
the first thinkers of ancient Greece toward an undif-
ferentiated world of science, wisdom, and poetry. Common
sense and the spontaneous pervasiveness of natural insight
and reasoning constitute the dynamic unity of the adolescent's universe of thought, before wisdom may achieve in
man a stabler unity. Just as imagination was the mental
heaven of childhood, so now ascending reason, natural
reason with its freshness, boldness, and first sparkling am-
bitions, is the mental heaven of adolescence; it is with
reasoning that adolescence happens to be intoxicated. Here
is a natural impulse to be turned to account by education,
both by stimulating and by disciplining reason.

Such are, to my mind, the considerations which should
guide the teachers of youth in the most important and
difficult part of their task, which consists in determining
the *mode* in which the instruments of thought and the
liberal arts are to be taught. The quality of the mode or

style is of much greater moment than the quantity of things taught, it constitutes the very soul of teaching and preserves its unity and makes it alive and buoyant. If we seek to characterize the general objective of instruction at the stage of college education, we might say the objective is less the acquisition of science itself or art itself than the grasp of their *meaning* and the comprehension of the truth or beauty they yield. It is less a question of sharing in the very activity of the scientist or the poet than of nourishing oneself intellectually on the results of their achievement. Still less is it a question of developing one's own mental skill and taste in the fashion of the dilettante by gaining a superficial outlook on scientific or artistic procedures or the ways and means, the grammar, logic, methodology thereof. What I call the *meaning* of a science or art is contained in the specific truth or beauty it offers us. The objective of education is to see to it that the youth grasps this truth or beauty by the natural power and gifts of his mind and the natural intuitive energy of his reason backed up by his whole sensuous, imaginative, and emotional dynamism. In doing that a liberal education will cause his natural intelligence to follow in the footsteps of those intellectual virtues which are the eminent merit of the real scientist or artist. The practical condition for all that is to strive to penetrate as deeply as possible into the great achievements of the human mind rather than to tend toward material erudition and atomized memorization. So I should say that the youth is to learn and know music in order to understand the meaning of music rather than in order to become a composer. He must learn and know physics in order to understand the meaning of physics rather than to become a physicist. Thus college education can keep its necessary character of comprehensive universality and at the same time till and cultivate the whole mind, made available and alive, for the tasks of man.

The Universal Character of Liberal Education

In a social order fitted to the common dignity of man, college education should be given to all,* so as to complete the preparation of the youth before he enters the state of manhood. To introduce specialization in this sphere is to do violence to the world of youth. As a matter of fact, a young man will choose his specialty for himself and progress all the more rapidly and perfectly in vocational, scientific, or technical training in proportion as his education has been liberal and universal. Youth has a right to education in the liberal arts, in order to be prepared for human work and for human leisure. But such education is killed by premature specialization.†

No doubt, a certain amount of specialization is to take place progressively, as the youth, leaving the public school and advancing into college education, gradually takes on the dimensions of a man. But this kind of specialization is merely that which the temperament, gifts, and inclinations of the youth himself spontaneously provide. Here we may observe that exacting from all pupils

* ". . . Since liberal education is the sort that enables each man to think as well as his native powers permit, it is by definition appropriate to all men. It is not for the rich alone, nor the intellectual élite alone. . . . A free society that limits it to a small fraction of its citizens, does so at the peril of its existence." S. Barr, *Report of the President,* July 1942, St. John's College, Annapolis, Maryland, p. 14.

† "Since to live well, since even to earn a living, requires a man to think, liberal education is the basic preparation for life. But it is a full-time job and cannot be carried on adequately by institutions that attempt simultaneously to give occupational training and what they may call 'practical' knowledge. That kind of knowledge can be speedily acquired, whether on the job or in a post-graduate professional school, by the man who has learned to think. It can be acquired only with difficulty and inadequately by the man who has not. The penalty which contemporary society has paid for omitting this basic sort of education is the multiplication of highly trained specialists, who are, fundamentally, uneducated men and who are inadequate to the varied responsibilities of life." *Ibid.*

the same degree of rigorous study and progress in all items of the curriculum is most unwise. If the youth displays eagerness with regard to certain matters, even a natural apathy in regard to others will be a normal mode of differentiation. Laziness must be fought, of course, but encouraging and urging a youth on the ways which he likes and in which he succeeds is much more important, providing, however, that he be also trained in the things for which he feels less inclination, and that he traverses the entire field of those human possibilities and achievements which compose liberal education.

The conclusion of all the preceding remarks implies a clear condemnation not only of the many preprofessional undergraduate courses which worm their way into college education but also of the elective system.*

* "The child-centered school may be attractive to the child, and no doubt is useful as a place in which the little ones may release their inhibitions and hence behave better at home. But educators cannot permit the students to dictate the course of study unless they are prepared to confess that they are nothing but chaperons, supervising an aimless, trial-and-error process which is chiefly valuable because it keeps young people from doing something worse. The free elective system as Mr. Eliot introduced it at Harvard and as Progressive Education adapted it to lower age levels amounted to a denial that there was content to education. Since there was no content to education, we might as well let students follow their own bent. They would at least be interested and pleased and would be as well educated as if they had pursued a prescribed course of study. This overlooks the fact that the aim of education is to connect man with man, to connect the present with the past, and to advance the thinking of the race. If this is the aim of education, it cannot be left to the sporadic, spontaneous interests of children or even of undergraduates." Robert M. Hutchins, *The Higher Learning in America* (Yale University Press, 1936), pp. 70–71

Of course, the rejection of the elective system does not imply that in addition to the essential (and therefore required) subjects of the curriculum other subjects should not be taught in optional courses, chosen by students according to their own preferences.

Be it noted that the age and degree of maturity of the student is a factor to be considered, and that any discussion of the elective system would be made easier and clearer if college years began earlier than is the case today, and extended from sixteen to nineteen.

The Curriculum

If all this is true, what can we say now about the curriculum? In touching on this question my purpose is only to seek, from a philosophical point of view and with respect solely to the intrinsic requirements and suitabilities of the task of bringing up a man, what would be the main features of a *normal* college curriculum, for a Western youth of our day.

I advance the opinion, incidentally, that, in the general educational scheme, it would be advantageous to hurry the four years of college, so that the period of undergraduate studies would extend from sixteen to nineteen. Thus, after the years of secondary education, dealing primarily with national and foreign languages (which should be learned from early youth),* comparative grammar, history, natural history and the art of expression,† we would have the following for the four years of undergraduate school, dur-

---

* Supposing that the training in foreign languages begins at the age of ten, the youth will have a sufficient mastery of these languages after six years of training. At sixteen, in his freshman year at college, he will bring this knowledge to completion in regard to the sphere of the humanities, with a rational and logical analysis of what he has already studied more or less empirically.

† Supposing that the period of the humanities were to last seven years, so that secondary education, which forms the transition between the period of rudiments and the college, and whose importance is therefore crucial, would comprise three years (from thirteen to fifteen), we might order these three years as follows:

The year of *Languages,* comprising: first, foreign languages, studied in connection with the national language; second, comparative grammar and the art of expression; third, national history, geography, and natural history (especially elementary astronomy and geology).

The year of *Grammar,* comprising: first, grammar, especially comparative grammar and philology; second, foreign languages and the art of expression; third, national history, geography, natural history (especially botany).

The year of *History and Expression,* comprising: first, national history, history of civilization, the art of expression; second, foreign languages;

ing which the student enters and encompasses the universe of liberal arts:

The year of *Mathematics and Poetry*, comprising: first, mathematics, and literature and poetry; second, logic; third, foreign languages, and the history of civilization.

The year of *Natural Sciences and Fine Arts*, comprising: first, physics and natural science; second, fine arts, mathematics, literature and poetry; third, history of the sciences.

The year of *Philosophy* comprising: first, philosophy, that is to say, metaphysics and philosophy of nature, theory of knowledge, psychology; second, physics and natural science; third, mathematics, literature and poetry, fine arts.

The year of *Ethical and Political Philosophy*, compris-

third, comparative grammar and philology, geography, natural history (especially zoölogy).

Thus the field of what I called in my second chapter *the pre-liberal arts* would be covered in the three years of secondary education (with the exception of logic which would be studied in the first year of college).

The general plan which I have in mind and which forms the background of my present considerations divides the main educational periods as follows: I. The rudiments (or elementary education): 7 years, divided into 4 years of initial elementary education (age: six to nine) and 3 years of complementary elementary education (age: ten to twelve). II. The humanities: 7 years, divided into 3 years of secondary education or high school (age: thirteen to fifteen) and 4 years of college education (age: sixteen to nineteen.) III. Advanced studies, comprising the university and higher specialized learning.

The B.A. would be awarded at the end of the college years, as crowning the humanities and making possible admission to the university. There, the time normally required for the M.A. would be 3 years; and for the Ph.D., roughly from 2 to 4 years. This general plan seems to be in substantial agreement with the reforms proposed by Professor John U. Nef in *The United States and Civilization,* chap ix, and by President Robert Hutchins in *Education for Freedom,* chap. iv. Yet, since the four years of college would be hurried, the B.A. would be awarded at the end of the senior year, according to the tradition, and not at the end of the sophomore year. The result would be the same with regard to the age of the student.

ing: first, ethics, political and social philosophy; second, physics and natural science; third, mathematics, literature and poetry, fine arts, history of civilization and history of the sciences.*

I note that up to this year of ethical and political philosophy, morality, both personal and social, should have been the object of a particular teaching all through the period of the humanities. May I confess at this point that, although I believe in natural morality, I feel little trust in the educational efficacy of any merely rational moral teaching abstractly detached from its religious environment? Normally, the moral teaching of which I just spoke as contradistinguished from ethical and political philosophy, and which is to be given all through the period of the humanities, should, in my opinion, be embodied in religious training. What, however, is to be done about natural morality? Natural morality and the great ethical ideas conveyed by civilization should be taught during these years. They are the very treasure of classical humanism, they must be communicated to the youth, but not as a subject of special courses. They should be embodied in the humanities and liberal arts, especially as an integral part of the teaching of literature, poetry, fine arts, and history. This teaching should be permeated with the feeling for such values. The reading of Homer, Aeschylus, Sophocles, Herodotus, Thucydides, Demosthenes, Plutarch, Epictetus, Marcus Aurelius (better to read them carefully in translation than to learn their language and to read only bits), the reading of Virgil, Terence, Tacitus and Cicero, of Dante, Cervantes, Shakespeare, Pascal, Racine, Montesquieu, Gibbon, Goethe, Dostoevski, feeds the mind with the sense and knowledge

* As I indicate farther on, the curriculum of the last two or three college years would also comprise optional studies in theology. See pages 73–75.

of natural virtues, of honor and pity, of the dignity of man and of the spirit, the greatness of human destiny, the entanglements of good and evil, the *caritas humani generis*. Such reading, more than any course in natural ethics, conveys to the youth the moral experience of mankind.

Commenting upon our ideal curriculum, a few remarks may be offered. As I pointed out in the previous lecture, physics and natural science must be considered as one of the chief branches of liberal arts. They are mainly concerned with the mathematical reading of natural phenomena, and insure in this way the domination of the human spirit over the world of matter, not in terms of ontological causes but rather in terms of number and measurement. Thus they appear, so to speak, as a final realization of the Pythagorean and Platonist trends of thought in the very field of that world of experience and the becoming which Plato looked at as a shadow on the wall of the cave. Physics and natural science, if they are taught not only for the sake of practical applications but essentially for the sake of knowledge, with reference to the specific epistemological approach they involve and in close connection with the history of the sciences and the history of civilization, provide man with a vision of the universe and an understanding of scientific truth and a sense of the sacred, exacting, unbending objectivity of the humblest truth, which play an essential part in the liberation of the mind and in liberal education. Physics should be taught and revered as a liberal art of the first rank, like poetry, and probably more important than even mathematics.

Our curriculum, besides, does not mention either Latin or Greek; in my opinion, they would represent chiefly a waste of time for the many destined to forget them; Latin, Greek, and Hebrew (or at least one of these three root-languages of our civilization) should be learned later on—

much more rapidly and fruitfully—by graduate students in languages, literature, history or philosophy. During the humanities, moreover, comparative grammar and philology* would provide the student with a most useful knowledge of the inner mechanisms of language. And foreign languages, studied not only for practical purposes but also in connection with the national language, would afford the required means of gaining mastery over the latter (particularly through exercises of translation).

Finally, as for literature and poetry, the direct reading and study of books written by great authors is the primary educational means; this point has been clearly brought to light by the educators of St. John's College. Nothing can replace the "pure reading," as Charles Péguy put it, of a "pure text." Such reading is also essential in philosophy, and even, in some measure, in sciences. This nevertheless, it seems to me, is all the more profitable as the books in question are not too many in number and therefore may be seriously and lovingly scrutinized, and as they depend, I mean in part, on the free choice of the student.†

* According to our general scheme, comparative grammar and philology should be taught—as instruments rather than as sciences, and in a manner fitted to the sphere of knowledge of the young—before the college, during the years of secondary education.

† In an address on "The Order of Learning" (reprinted from *The Moraga Quarterly,* autumn, 1941), Professor Mortimer J. Adler made many interesting statements and criticisms which should be discussed at this point. For brevity's sake, I shall advance only the following remarks.

(1). One cannot emphasize too much the educational role of great books. Yet this role does not only consist in sharpening the intellectual power of the youth; they are not only like a large bone with which a puppy struggles so that his teeth may grow sharper. To bring the metaphor to completion, it should be added that this large bone is a marrowbone, and that not only do the puppy's teeth have to grow sharper, but his living substance also has to feed itself on the valuable marrow. It is doubtless not a question for the young student of "mastering" the great books, but of discovering and being quickened and delighted by

Philosophy and Theology

A last observation must be made, that deals with the highest aim of liberal education which is to make youth possess the foundations of wisdom. At this point I need

the truth and beauty they convey—and, if they convey errors too, of discerning and judging the latter, however awkward and imperfect this process may be at first. The intellect's teeth are not really sharpened if they are not able to separate the true from the false. That is why the great books should not be too many in number, and their reading should be accompanied by enlightenment about their historical context and by courses on the subject matter.

(2). College education does not aim at having intellectual virtues gained by the youth in a state of possession, but only in a state of *preparation*. Arts and sciences are to be really acquired only in the third stage of education (university, specialized advanced studies). The reason why college education must embrace *all liberal arts*, as required for all, is precisely the fact that it is only concerned with the comprehension thereof by the youth's *natural* intelligence, progressing in this way toward the *habitus* or virtues.

(3). The traditional expression "liberal arts" must be correctly understood. In this expression the word "art" does not mean art in its strict sense, as contradistinguished from "knowledge" or "science." On the contrary, it relates to the liberal achievements of the mind in general, comprising both art and knowledge. Thus, in the Middle Ages, the mathematical sciences (arithmetic and geometry) and the physical sciences (astronomy and music, that is, acoustics) were the main arts of the quadrivium. Therefore education in the liberal arts is not only an education in the practical or "artistic" rules of good thinking, or in a perfect sharpening of the teeth (that is to say, an attainment of indispensable *means*), it is also and mainly an education in knowledge and insight, and in a real grasping of truth and beauty (that is to say, an attainment—proportionate to the universe of thought of the youth— of those *ends* of the intellectual effort which are the various subject matters).

(4). Logic should be taught (with mathematics and literature and poetry) during the first college year. On this point my plan is in agreement with the observations of Mortimer Adler. What I mean by logic, however, is what the late Scholastics called *logica minor* (both an instrumental science and an art, dealing with the rules of reasoning). What they called *logica major,* and the study of what is logic itself and what is its object, should be taught, as Adler points out in other words, together with the theory of knowledge, in the last college year.

(5). Mortimer Adler rightly insists that the order of teaching (parnot dwell on the vindication of philosophy. It is enough to repeat a remark often made indeed, namely that nobody can do without philosophy, and that, after all, the only way of avoiding the damage wrought by an unconscious belief in a formless and prejudiced philosophy is to develop a philosophy consciously. Furthermore metaphysics is the only human knowledge which actually claims to be wisdom, and to have such penetration and universality that it can actually bring the realm of the sciences into unity, coöperation, and accord; and if anybody honestly wishes to dispute the validity of this claim, he must perforce begin by knowing the metaphysics that he challenges. In fine, education deals ultimately with the great achievements of the human mind; and without knowing philosophy and the achievements of the great thinkers it is utterly impossible for us to understand anything of the development of mankind, civilization, culture, and science.

There is, in this connection, a really difficult question. A good philosophy should be a true philosophy. Now the professors of philosophy are bound to hold philosophical positions which differ widely. And if one of these positions is grounded in true principles, apparently the others are not. The solution for this problem may take two forms. First, there is a common, though unformulated,

ticularly during the first two stages of education) should follow the order of discovery, which is not primarily "deductive and scientific" but rather "inductive and dialectical." Of course some dialectics is good, and the Socratic training in the comparison of ideas very useful, but as regards the development of the critical mind rather than the way of discovery. I wonder why Mortimer Adler directs his criticism against the *Posteriora Analytica* of Aristotle and not against the Platonic dialectics, which remain imbued with the assumption that knowledge is innate in us and that we can discover it by merely dividing and comparing and struggling with our ideas. Educational emphasis on dialectics is no better than educational emphasis on the syllogism. The order of discovery—and therefore the order of teaching—is experiential-inductive and rational-intuitive rather than inductive and dialectical.

heritage of philosophical wisdom which passes through any real teaching of philosophy, whatever may be the system of the teacher. Reading Plato is ever a blessing, even if you disagree with the tenets of Platonism. Second, teachers in philosophy are not teaching to be believed but in order to awaken reason; and the students in philosophy owe it to their teacher to free themselves from him. There is indeed a third point, which is valid only for philosophers as hardened as myself: they may always hope, indeed, that by virtue of its very truth, the philosophy which they think to be true, as I do Aristotelian and Thomistic philosophy, will gain momentum among their fellow men, at least in the generation to come.

A further question may be posed concerning the ways of teaching philosophy. The difficulty, here, lies in the fact that philosophy starts from experience, and that there is in young men no experience, or very little, either in science or in life, fitted to provide a starting point. One remedy consists, to my mind, in beginning by giving historical enlightenment with regard to the great problems in philosophy: such a historical description, pointing less at history than at making clear the inner logic and development of the human awareness of these problems, is a kind of vicarious personal experience.

Now, those who share in the Christian creed know that another rational wisdom, which is rooted in faith, not in reason alone, is superior to the merely human wisdom of metaphysics. As a matter of fact, theological problems and controversies have permeated the whole development of Western culture and civilization, and are still at work in its depths, in such a way that the one who would ignore them would be fundamentally unable to grasp his own time and the meaning of its internal conflicts. Thus impaired, he would be like a barbarous and disarmed child walking amidst the queer and incomprehensible trees, fountains, statues, gardens, ruins, and buildings still under construction, of the old park of civilization. The intellectual and political history of the sixteenth, seventeenth and eighteenth centuries, the Reformation and the Counter Reformation, the internal state of British society after the Revolution in England, the achievements of the Pilgrim Fathers, the Rights of Man, and the further events in world history have their starting point in the great disputes on nature and grace of our classical age. Neither Dante nor Cervantes nor Rabelais nor Shakespeare nor John Donne nor William Blake, nor even Oscar Wilde or D. H. Lawrence, nor Giotto nor Michelangelo nor El Greco nor Zurbaran, nor Pascal nor Rousseau, nor Madison nor Jefferson nor Edgar Allan Poe nor Baudelaire, nor Goethe nor Nietzsche nor even Karl Marx, nor Tolstoy nor Dostoevski is actually understandable without a serious theological background. Modern philosophy itself, from Descartes to Hegel, remains enigmatic without that, for in actual fact philosophy has burdened itself all through modern times with problems and anxieties taken over from theology, so that the cultural advent of a philosophy purely philosophical is still to be waited for. In the cultural life of the Middle Ages philosophy was subservient to theology or rather wrapped up in it; in that of modern times it was but secularized theology. Thus the considerations I have laid down regarding philosophy are still truer of theology. Nobody can do without theology, at least a concealed and unconscious theology, and the best way of avoiding the inconveniences of an insinuated theology is to deal with theology that is consciously aware of itself. And liberal education cannot complete its task without the knowledge of the specific realm and the concerns of theological wisdom.

As a result, a theological course should be given during

the last two or three years of study of the humanities—
a course which by its sharply intellectual and speculative
nature is quite different from the religious training
received by the youth in another connection.

The practical aspect of this question is of no difficulty
for denominational colleges.* With regard to nondenominational colleges, the practical solution would depend on
the recognition of a pluralist principle in such matters.
Theological teaching would be given, according to the
diversity of creeds, by professors belonging to the main
religious denominations, each one addressing the students
of his own denomination. And of course, those students
who nurture a bias against theology would be released from
attending these courses and allowed to remain incomplete
in wisdom at their own pleasure.

3. THE UNIVERSITY

The Architecture of an Ideal University

The third and advanced stage in education concerns the
young man and woman. These have already entered the
adult universe of thought and are preparing themselves at
close range for the tasks of manhood and womanhood.
They enjoy the first hopes and experiences of their coming of age, and of self-determination due to reason and
free will already shaped. The life and concerns of the mature world are now theirs. Marriage will come shortly for
most of them. Perhaps in some ideal future society all
youth—I mean those who possess the required gifts and
eagerness—will have the possibility of being only concerned with advanced training until their twenty-fifth or
twenty-sixth year. Yet, as a matter of fact, many now are

* Cf. Dr. Gerald B. Phelan's indisputable statement on "Theology in
the Curriculum of Catholic Colleges and Universities," in *Man and Secu-
larism* (National Catholic Alumni Association, New York, 1940), pp.
128–140.

obliged to work full time in order to earn their living. If, according to the European habit, we reserve the name university for higher learning in advanced and graduate studies, we might say that the aim of the university is to achieve the formation and equipment of the youth in regard to the strength and maturity of judgment and the intellectual virtues. As Cardinal Newman puts it, a university "is a place of *teaching* universal *knowledge.*" He adds: "Whatever was the original reason of its adoption, which is unknown, I am only putting on its popular, its recognized sense, when I say that a University should teach universal knowledge." *

Yet, paradoxically enough, university teaching coincides with a definite specialization of studies. Each particular science and art demands a highly specialized training. And in our age, when such teaching does not deal, as in the Middle Ages, with the formation of an intellectual leadership essentially consisting of clerics, nor, as in the following centuries, with the formation of the potential members of the ruling classes, but deals, according to a more democratic pattern, with the formation of a much larger and more diversified mass of outstanding citizens of all ranks in the nation, it is suitable that actually all the arts and sciences, even those which concern the management of common life and the application of the human mind to matters of practical utility, should be embraced by the typical modern university. The latter would thus have its field of specialization multiplied still more, as well as the number and diversity of its courses, a very small part of which each particular student can attend. The university should nevertheless still keep its essential character of universality,† and teach universal

---

* Cardinal John Henry Newman, *On the Scope and Nature of University Education,* Preface and Discourse I.

† "For those whose formal education is prolonged beyond the school

knowledge, universal not only because all the parts of human knowledge would be represented in its architecture of teaching but also because this very architecture would have been planned according to the qualitative and internal hierarchy of human knowledge, and because from the bottom to the top, the arts and sciences would have been grouped and organized according to their growing value in spiritual universality.

Thus a first order of subjects would be concerned with the realm of useful arts and applied sciences in the broadest sense of these words, and with advanced studies in technical training, engineering, administrative sciences, arts and crafts, agriculture, mining, applied chemistry, statistics, commerce, finance, and so on.*

A second order would be the realm of those practical sciences—practical either because they belong to the domain of art or because they belong to the domain of ethics—which, though covering thoroughly specialized

age, the University course or its equivalent is the great period of generalization. The spirit of generalization should dominate a University. . . . At the University the student should start from general ideas and study their applications to concrete cases. A well-planned University course is a study of the wide sweep of generality. I do not mean that it should be abstract in the sense of divorce from concrete fact, but that concrete fact should be studied as illustrating the scope of general ideas." A. N. Whitehead, *The Aims of Education and Other Essays* (The Macmillan Co., New York, 1929), p. 41.

* With regard to this first order of subjects, as well as to the second, it is to be emphasized that the reason for teaching such subjects in the university and the viewpoint from which they should be ordered and organized as part of the university curriculum must remain solely the *universality of knowledge*. It is as parts of the manifold body of human knowledge and for the sake of (practical) truth that they have to be taught and organized. Everything would be warped if the aim, incentive, and dominating concern of the teaching were directed toward success in the experiences of life and in money-making. The students may take such motives into consideration when they choose to enter a given course of study. But the curriculum itself must be directed only toward a sound and comprehensive organization of universal knowledge, to be taught according to the internal and objective structure of the parts thereof.

fields, nevertheless relate to man himself and human life; medicine and psychiatry, for instance, and, on the other hand, law, economics and politics, education, etc.

A third order would be the realm of the speculative sciences and fine arts, in other words it would be concerned with the liberal arts proper and with that disinterested knowledge of nature and man and of the achievements of culture which liberates the mind by truth or beauty. At this point we find the immense chorus of the free workings of the spirit, mathematics, physics, chemistry, astronomy, geology, biology, anthropology, psychology, prehistory, archeology, history, ancient and modern literature and languages, philology, music, fine arts, and so on. That is the very core of the life of the university and the very treasure of the civilized heritage. And this third order is to culminate in a fourth one, which is the highest animating center in the architecture of teaching, and which deals with those sciences that are also wisdom because they are universal by virtue of their very object and of their very essence: the philosophy of nature, metaphysics and the theory of knowledge, ethical philosophy, social and political philosophy, the philosophy of culture and of history, theology and the history of religions.

In such an ideal university, I see the diverse parts of the vast body of teaching divided into Institutes, each one possessing its own complex organization and being organically linked to the others, rather than into separate Departments or Faculties. The Institutes of the first order would compose a teaching City concerned with the technical means of human life, or with the practical domination and utilization of matter. Those of the second order would compose a City concerned with the means which deal with human life itself for its maintenance and improvement. The Institutes of the third order would compose a teaching City of pure knowledge concerned with the intellectual ends of human life which are reached by encompassing in the mind the manifold universe of nature and man and the achievements of human creative power. The Institutes of the fourth order would compose a teaching City of the higher and intrinsically universal knowledge concerned with those intellectual ends of human life which are reached by grasping the trans-sensible realm of Being, Spirit, and Divine Reality, and the ethical realm of the aims, conditions, and rational ordering of human freedom and conduct.

The Consummation of Liberal Education

Obviously it is not enough that the universality of knowledge and the superior unity of intrinsically universal sciences be embodied in the general architecture of such teaching Cities. It is also necessary that in some measure they actually inspire the intellectual development of that living subject, the student, and become for him an integral part of him, whatever the special requirements of his course may be. Here we are confronted with the main duty and the main difficulty of university teaching.

The universe of thought we are contemplating in this last stage of formal education is in process of definite differentiation and formulation. Judgment and the intellectual virtues are no longer in the stage of preparation but in the stage of actual acquisition. And it is then, as I pointed out, that specialization necessarily occurs. The intellectual virtues acquired by one student are not those acquired by another, be it a question of techniques, useful arts, and applied sciences, or of practical sciences dealing with human life or of speculative sciences. The knowledge which has to develop during university years is knowledge in a state of a *perfected and rational grasping* of a particular subject matter. Truth, which is the mental atmosphere and the inspiring force needed more than ever, is henceforth an objectively circumscribed truth, speculative or practical, at which each of the diverse sciences and arts aims.

How is it possible to assure at this stage the universal inspiration and mental comprehensiveness of which I just spoke? An organic coöperation will be necessary between the diverse Institutes of the university; there will be required of each student, whatever his special training may be, a measure of general training in those subjects which constitute the very core of university life and with which our third and fourth orders of teaching are concerned. As a matter of fact, the use of technical means cannot be really profitable, nor the practical sciences be well directed without general enlightenment about nature and man. Medicine, public sanitation, psychiatry are extrinsically—law, sociology, economics and politics, pedagogy are intrinsically—subordinated to ethics and natural law, and the very truth of every knowledge bearing on human conduct implies sound judgment about the ends of human life, that is to say the actual knowledge of ethical and political philosophy, which in its turn presupposes metaphysics. These requirements proceed from the very objects on which knowledge shapes itself. Even the scientist, as well as the historian, the scholar and humanist, the artist, cannot dispense with some philosophical inspiration; they need philosophical instruction, at least in order to be aware of the exact value and legitimate extent of their own activities among others of the spirit.

As a result, each university student should be required to attend a certain number of courses in the teaching Cities of pure knowledge and universal knowledge. Part of these courses, for instance in science, history, ancient and modern literatures, or fine arts, would be a matter of free choice, according to the personal inclination of the student, and to the need for complement or contrast in his special training. Other courses should be required for all, namely general philosophy, ethical and political philosophy, the history of civilization.

But, as Professor Nef rightly observes, such a measure would remain insufficient if it were not completed by an organic structure embodying that sense of unity and universality which should pervade university life. Special committees, composed of professors belonging to various Institutes, should ensure regular coöperation between these Institutes, guide the work of the student and help him scrutinize the connections of his own particular subject with other and more universal fields of higher learning: for instance, the connections of physics, biology, psychology, or medicine with the history of the sciences, the history of civilization, the philosophy of nature, and the theory of knowledge; or the connections of economics, social science, law, education, or of literature and art, with the history of civilization, ethical and political philosophy, and the great metaphysical and theological problems. Thus would be facilitated "study and research in which several disciplines, now separated, would be combined both by students working for higher degrees and by mature scholars in their creative labors." * And the knowledge of each one would be deepened and vitalized by the reëxamination

* John U. Nef, *The Universities Look for Unity*, p. 36. The author wisely says that, in order to succeed in this progressive work of recasting, "unification could begin modestly, where the need for it appeared, between two or three subjects, considered in so far as possible in relation to philosophy and particularly to ethics" *idem*, p. 37. In connection with these remarks, the initiative taken by the Committee on Social Thought of the University of Chicago is to be pointed out. In order to have the Master's and Doctor's degrees prepared under its guidance, this interdepartmental committee combines in various ways courses of study such as social thought, historical fields (ancient Near Eastern civilizations, Far Eastern civilizations, medieval civilization, Renaissance civilization, eighteenth-century civilization, American civilization) and analytical and theoretical fields (anthropology and sociology, politics, economics, jurisprudence and ethics, education, psychology, and human development.)

of the value, purpose and logical structure proper to the various disciplines vitally brought together in this way.

For the reasons which I stated above apropos of the humanities, courses in theology, however important in themselves, would be a matter of free choice. Of course the question of theological teaching crops up with regard to the university as well as with regard to college education, and the considerations we previously laid down in this connection are here of special moment. Those who believe that God revealed to mankind His intimate secrets hold theology, or the rational development and penetration of the revealed data, to be in itself real knowledge in the strict sense of the term, though it is rooted in faith and grasps its object by means of concepts which are infinitely transcended and exceeded by it. In order to make philosophy autonomous, Descartes deemed it necessary to consider faith mere obedience, and to refuse to see any character of real knowledge in theology. Thus he threw out the baby with the bath. I am convinced that one of the main tasks of our age is to recognize both the distinction and the organic relationship between theology, rooted in faith, and philosophy, rooted in reason, and now secure of its sought-for autonomy. For it is not likely, is it, that if God spoke, it was to say nothing to human intelligence? From this point of view, Newman was right in stating that if a university professes it to be its scientific duty to exclude theology from its curriculum, "such an Institution cannot be what it professes, if there be a God."

As for the many who do not share in these feelings about theology, they would nevertheless derive great advantage from theological instruction. They would gain horizons of highly rationalized problems thus opened up to them, and better understand the roots of our culture and civilization.

In nondenominational universities, this theological teaching would be divided into Institutes of diverse religious affiliation, according to the student population of the university. Such teaching should remain thoroughly distinct from the one given in religious seminaries, and be adapted to the intellectual needs of laymen; its aim should not be to form a priest, a minister, or a rabbi, but to enlighten students of secular matters about the great doctrines and perspectives of theological wisdom. The history of religions should form an important part of the curriculum.

I spoke a while ago of the large category of young men and women who after the college years (supposedly made accessible to all) must dedicate their entire day to earning a living. Those among them who are gifted and eager for intellectual work are thus made unable, whatever may be their personal desires, to become regular university students. For such a sad anomaly scholarships and grants can make up to a certain extent—they should be multiplied as far as possible. Yet the only way in which this anomaly can be compensated for in a general manner consists of extension courses and evening courses. The generosity and eagerness with which such teaching is given by so many professors and received by so many students, after a hard day of work, is one of the finest achievements of American education. There appears here a new function in university life, and it is probable that this function is called upon to assume ever greater importance, in proportion as economic progress will generally reduce working time and thus enable those who want to do so to use more easily the facilities of evening courses.

The Institutes of Advanced Research

We may furthermore observe that the work of universities

must find its complement in the work of Institutes of Advanced Research. It is no doubt normal that any instruction given in the university will result in some original work and the advancement of knowledge, especially in science. Yet this is in a way an overflow of the teaching scholarship. In the nature of things, the object of universities is the teaching of youth, and not producing books and articles and endless contributions, or making some scientific, philosophical, or artistic discovery. Man's education by means of courses, seminars, and laboratory training, on the one hand, and the advancement of knowledge through original enquiry, which implies both concentration and the "beautiful risks" of which Plato spoke, are two quite different things—we professors know this all too well. Specially organized and endowed Institutes of Research delving into the sciences of nature and of man have outstanding importance for the progress of civilization: they and the universities should help one another, but they should remain, for their mutual advantage, clearly distinct.

The Schools in Spiritual Life

Another complement, relating to quite a different purpose, might also be considered.

In China and India, wise men living in solitude and contemplation gather together disciples who come to listen to them either for a certain number of years or at certain seasons of the year. The Hindu *ashrams* or schools of wisdom are well known. In Europe, some years ago, the need for such places of spiritual enlightenment was so great that schools of wisdom were created here and there, even by men who perhaps, like Spengler, hardly deserved the name of wise men. Here in America, the initiative taken by the Quakers with their school at Pendle Hill is to be considered with special interest. For centuries the Catho-

lic Church has had its own means of instructing those
who aspire to spiritual perfection.* My point is that special initiatives have always been taken and must be taken
according to the special needs of each time.

I do not feel qualified to discuss the matter from
any outlook other than that of my own religious affiliation.
Speaking therefore from the Catholic point of view, I
should like to say that what seems to me to be especially
required by our time is the creation of centers of spiritual
enlightenment, or schools of wisdom, in which those interested in spiritual life would be able to lead a common life
during some weeks, to be trained in the ways of spiritual
life and contemplation, and to learn that science of evan-
gelical perfection which is the highest part of theology.
The immense treasure of the writings and doctrines of the
great spiritual authors and the saints, which compose the
mystical tradition of Christendom, from the Desert
Fathers to St. John of the Cross and the mystics of modern
times, would thus be made available to them. They would
become acquainted both with the theological knowledge
concerned and with the history, personality, and teachings
of those heroes of faith and love whose call, according to
Henri Bergson, passes through mankind as a powerful
"aspiration" toward God. I conceive of these schools as
houses of hospitality and enlightenment for human souls,
which would be grounded on the integrity of a given religious faith and way of life, but which would be open not
only to those sharing in this faith but also to all who
desire to spend some days of spiritual refreshment there
and to learn what they are ignorant of. People who assure
the continuity of life and teaching in these schools of wisdom would stay there permanently. The others would be

* This is the aim of its religious orders, its confraternities of laymen
connected with them, its spiritual retreats, and its innumerable activities of spiritual guidance.

guests, meeting each other at regular periods. As concerns youth especially, the university students, and the other boys and girls who enjoy a period of vacation and would like to use part of it in this manner, might spend some days or some weeks in such places of peace. I guess that the number of students in these schools would not be small.

Our Responsibility toward Youth

Thus we have completed our considerations of the humanities and liberal education. The next chapter will be concerned with the educational problems of our day, with regard to the present crisis of civilization and postwar needs. At this point I should like to stress that it is above all in thinking of the needs, exigencies, and rights of youth, and especially of contemporary youth, that I have discussed the entire subject. I like and respect contemporary youth, and I contemplate them with a strange feeling of anguish. They know a great deal about matter, natural facts, and human facts, but almost nothing about the soul. All in all, their moral standard is not lower, though more openly lax, than that of the preceding generation. They have a sort of confident candor which rends the heart. At first glance they appear close to the goodness of nature as Rousseau dreamed of it. For they are good indeed and generous and free, and they even display, in noble as well as in immoral deeds, a kind of purity which resembles the innocence of birds and deer. In reality they are just at that stage where the acquired structures of moral and religious tradition have been taken away, and man still remains playing with his heritage. Their naked nature is not mere nature, but nature which for centuries had been strengthened by reason and faith and accustomed to virtues, and which is now stripped of every prop. They stand in goodness upon nothing. How will they be tested in the hard world of tomorrow? What will their children be? Anxiety and thirst arise in a number of them, and this very fact is a reason for hope. Yet in tortured Europe the same youth is now torn between hopeless cynicism and heroic faith, while bodies are starving and souls agonizing in the face of persecution, betrayal, and ignominy.

THE TRIALS OF PRESENT-DAY EDUCATION

IN this last chapter we shall consider some of the tasks and trials with which education is confronted today. First I shall have to stress the importance of liberal education with regard to a new humanism. Second, the special tasks which the world of tomorrow will demand of education, especially as regards moral teaching and the needs of the political community. Third, the difficult problems which the present crisis of civilization summons education to solve, especially as regards the mental perversion brought about by "education for death" and as regards the renewed inspiration of our own education.

1. LIBERAL EDUCATION AND THE NEW HUMANISM WE HOPE FOR

I should like first to insist that our vindication of liberal education is not only grounded on the essential value of man's education but also upon its value in meeting some specific needs of the immediate future.

An Integral Education for an Integral Humanism

If mankind overcomes the terrible threats of slavery and dehumanization which it faces today, it will thirst for a new humanism, and be eager to rediscover the integrity of man, and to avoid the cleavages from which the preceding age suffered so much. To correspond to this integral humanism, there should be an integral education—the main features of which I have tried to outline in these chapters.

Bourgeois individualism is done for. What will assume full importance for the man of tomorrow are the vital connections of man with society, that is, not only the social environment but also common work and common good. The problem is to replace the individualism of the bourgeois era not by totalitarianism or the sheer collectivism of the beehive but by a personalistic and communal civilization, grounded on human rights and satisfying the social aspirations and needs of man. Education must remove the rift between the social claim and the individual claim within man himself. It must therefore develop both the sense of freedom and the sense of responsibility, human rights and human obligations, the courage to take risks and exert authority for the general welfare and the respect for the humanity of each individual person.

The education of tomorrow must also bring to an end the cleavage between religious inspiration and secular activity in man, if it is true that an integral humanism would have as one of its main features an effort of sanctification of profane and secular existence. And the education of tomorrow must bring to an end, too, the cleavage between work or useful activity and the blossoming of spiritual life and disinterested joy in knowledge and beauty. Here we perceive the genuinely democratic character of the education of tomorrow. Everyone must work, or share in the burden of the social community, according to his own ability. But work is not an end in itself; work should afford leisure for the joy, expansion, and delight of the spirit.

Human Leisure and Liberal Education

The problem of human leisure, which mechanical and social progress had already made important before the war, is bound to become a particularly crucial problem in the world of tomorrow. Physical and mental relaxation, plays, movies, games, are good and necessary. Only that leisure however is suitable to what is most human in man, and is of greater worth than work itself, which consists of an expansion of our inner activities in enjoying the fruits of knowledge and beauty. Liberal education enables man to do so. Here we see one of the reasons why liberal education should be extended to all.* Be it noted, by the way, that children who are apathetic or reluctant as regards liberal education, without eagerness to learn or mental inquisitiveness, are not to be found among the poorer classes more than among the wealthy ones (the opposite is more often the case). Those who are acquainted with working youth and labor know that nowhere is a greater thirst for knowledge to be found, if only sufficient facilities are given them. This thirst for knowledge, for liberal knowledge, is one with the thirst for social liberation and coming of age. The education of tomorrow must provide the common man with the means for his personal fulfillment, not only with regard to his labor but also with regard to his social and political activities in the civil commonwealth, and to the activities of his leisure hours.

---

* No doubt Professor Nef is right in insisting that sheer uniformity is a bad pattern and that after elementary education a differentiation in the educational paths should take place according to the capacities, gifts, and inclinations of the child. *The United States and Civilization,* p. 303 and sq. The "four varieties of schooling" he proposes for youth between the ages of twelve and eighteen or twenty correspond to really characteristic psychological patterns, but they should first of all imply that all young people receive during this period a genuine *liberal education,* and that differences in schooling do not infringe upon the basic requirements of education in the humanities and the liberal arts. In other words, the essentials of the ideal curriculum outlined in the preceding chapter for secondary and college education should be maintained as *the same for all young people* of a free country, and the varieties of schooling should only amount to particular adaptations of and complementary additions to the basic curriculum. College education should be provided for all, and variety in schooling should be ensured by colleges diversified in orientation and level, the liberal character of which would nevertheless remain fundamentally the same.

2. SOME SPECIAL TASKS IMPOSED UPON EDUCATION WITH REGARD TO THE WORLD OF TOMORROW

The Normal Task of Education and Its Superadded Burdens

We come now to the special tasks which the present crisis of civilization and the conditions of the postwar world are to impose upon education. These tasks are manifold and momentous. As a result of the present disintegration of family life, of a crisis in morality and the break between religion and life, and finally of a crisis in the political state and the civic conscience, and the necessity for democratic states to rebuild themselves according to new patterns, there is a tendency, everywhere, to burden education with remedying all these deficiencies. This involves a risk of warping educational work, especially when immediate transformations are expected from its supposedly magic power. Yet extraneous burdens superadded to the normal task of education must be accepted for the sake of the general welfare.

In such a situation, the duty of educators is obviously twofold: they have both to maintain the essentials of humanistic education and to adapt them to the present requirements of the common good.

Education has its own essence and its own aims. This essence and these essential aims, which deal with the formation of man and the inner liberation of the human person, must be preserved, whatever the superimposed burdens may be. It is not a question of refusing the latter. But if they were taken up in the wrong way, so as to warp the essential human values of education; or if the school, conceived according to some totalitarian pattern as an organ of the political state, were to replace the free and normal agencies provided by nature and by God for the upbringing of man, then the common good, for the sake of which

the superadded burdens must be assumed, would be not ensured, but betrayed. The remedy would only have aggra-
vated the evil.

The Educational System and the State

It is to be expected that in the world of tomorrow
the educational system will take on ever-growing importance and amplitude, and become, still more than today,
the basic and crucial function of a civil community aware
of the dignity of the people, and of the destined rise of the
common man. Since we have here a matter of public interest, the state cannot hold itself aloof from it, and its help
as well as its supervision will be accordingly required.
Many changes in the present status of colleges and universities will probably take place. The number of educational institutions founded and supported by the state will
probably increase. All this is a normal process in itself. But
it must be brought about in freedom and for freedom, and
the relationship between state and school must be rightly
understood.

Here we face again the importance of the pluralist
principle, which grants to the manifold groups arising
from free association the greatest possible autonomy, and
bases the state's superior authority on the recognition of
the rights of these groups. As concerns the educational
system, the pluralist principle implies basically academic
freedom. Not only does it stress the right to found schools,
which is open to everyone qualified and complying with
the laws of the state. It also demands that diverse teaching
institutions be free to join with each other in several unions
or organizations which would be prevented by law from
encroaching upon the basic liberties of their members,
but could establish general regulations valid inside each
union. It is by the agreements concluded between the

state and some general board composed of the representatives of these unions (including the unions of schools and colleges supported by the state) that any justifiable intervention of the state in educational matters might take place.

An important role should be granted to the parents' associations, which would make their desires heard by the educational body and whose claims could counterbalance the demands of the state. The role of labor unions and other great economic or cultural organizations, which might possibly become the founders and trustees of a number of privately endowed teaching institutions, should also be taken into consideration.

Moral Teaching

If we consider more closely the added tasks which I have mentioned, the first has to do with the present crisis in morality. The task of moral re-education is really a matter of public emergency. Every serious observer recognizes the fact that children have not only to be trained in proper conduct, law observance, and politeness, but that this very training remains deficient and precarious if there is no genuine internal formation. That the teachers in public schools may not face unruliness and violence, moral authority must be recognized; and there must be a serious teaching of moral principles, I mean as grounded on truth rather than as suitable to social convenience. This surely involves more than the theory that children should first set free the instincts of primitive man in order to purge themselves of them.

Professor F. Clarke, Director of the Institute of Education at the University of London, recently advocated severity and authority in schools and colleges, and "the continual maintenance in education," as he puts it, "of stringency and tension, something analogous to the conditions of 'fitness' in the physical field."*

He even went so far as to say that "original sin may be more than an outworn theological dogma after all," and that "of all the needs of democracy, some abiding sense of the reality of original sin may yet prove to be the greatest." As a Catholic, I readily agree with him, while adding that an abiding sense of the reality of the internal power of regenerating grace and faith, hope, and charity, may prove to be even more necessary.

Yet what our present problem asks us to take into consideration is the large number of parents who are opposed to any religious education for their children. Here we are confronted anew with a peculiar task required today from the school system, and which is momentous. Additional emphasis should be brought to the teaching of natural morality. The normal way of giving this teaching, which is to have it embodied in the humanities, literature, and history, as I pointed out in my third chapter, does not suffice in the face of the tremendous degradation of ethical reason which is observable today. For the moment the evil seems more apparent in our ideas than in our conduct, I mean in still civilized countries. Exhausted and bewildered by dint of false and dehumanized philosophy, reason confesses its impotence to justify any ethical standards. To such a disease of human intelligence and conscience, special remedies should be given, not only through the badly needed revival of religious faith but also through a revival of the moral power of reason. Accordingly, if teachers may be found whose reason is healthier than that of their students, special teaching should be provided, in schools and colleges, for the principles of natural morality.

Let us observe at this point that the field in which natural morality feels most at home, and least deficient, is the

* F. Clarke, *A Review of Educational Thought* (London, 1942).

field of our temporal activities, or of political, civic, and social morality: because the virtues proper to this field are essentially natural ones, directed toward the good of civilization; whereas in the field of personal morality, the whole scope of the moral life cannot be comprehended by reason with regard to our real system of conduct in actual existence, without taking into account the supratemporal destiny of man. So the teaching of natural morality will naturally tend to lay stress on what may be called the ethics of political life and of civilization. Which is all to the good (for here it enjoys its maximum strength and practical truth) provided that it resist the temptation of neglecting or disparaging personal morality, which is the root of all morality. Above all it should resist the temptation of warping and perverting all its work by making itself a tool of the state to shape youth according to the collective pattern supposedly needed by the pride, greed, or myths of the earthly community.

Now, since we are dealing with morality and moral teaching, we must not overlook the practical truth which is of the greatest moment in this regard: as to the actual uprightness of the will and human conduct, knowledge and sound teaching are necessary but are surely not enough. In order for us rightly to judge what to do in a particular case, our reason itself depends on the uprightness of our will, and on the decisive movement of our very freedom. The melancholy saying of Aristotle, contrasting with the Socratic doctrine that virtue is only knowledge, is to be recalled in this connection: "To know," he said, "does little, or even nothing, for virtue."*

What does a great deal for virtue is love: because the basic hindrance to moral life is egoism, and the chief yearning of moral life liberation from oneself; and only

* II *Ethic.;* cf. Saint Thomas Aquinas, III *Sent.,* dist. 33, 9, 2.

love, being the gift of oneself, is able to remove this hindrance and to bring this yearning to fulfillment. But love itself is surrounded by our central egoism, and in perpetual danger of becoming entangled in and recaptured by it, whether this egoism makes the ones we love a prey to our devouring self-love or merges them in the ruthless self-love of the group, so as to exclude all other men from our love. Love does not regard ideas or abstractions or possibilities, love regards existing persons. God is the only person whom human love can fly to and settle in, so as to embrace also all other persons and be freed from egotistic self-love.

Love, human love as well as divine love, is not a matter of training or learning, for it is a gift; the love of God is a gift of nature and of grace: that is why it can be the first precept. How could we be commanded to put into action a power which we have not received or may not first receive? There are no human methods or techniques of getting or developing charity, any more than any other kind of love. There is nevertheless education in this matter: an education which is provided by trial and suffering, as well as by the human help and instruction of those whose moral authority is recognized by our conscience.

Here the educational sphere involved is first of all the family. Is not family love the primary pattern of any love uniting a community of men? Is not fraternal love the very name of that neighborly love which is but one with the love of God? No matter what deficiencies the family group may present in certain particular cases, no matter what trouble and disintegration the economic and social conditions of our day have brought to family life, the nature of things cannot be changed. And it is in the nature of things that the vitality and virtues of love develop first in the family. Not only the examples of the parents, and the rules of conduct which they inculcate, and the religious habits and inspiration which they further, and the memories of their own lineage which they convey, in short the educational work which they directly perform, but also, in a more general way, the common experiences and common trials, endeavors, sufferings, and hopes, and the daily labor of family life, and the daily love which grows up in the midst of cuffs and kisses, constitute the normal fabric where the feelings and the will of the child are naturally shaped. The society made up by his parents, his brothers and sisters, is the primary human society and human environment in which, consciously and subconsciously, he becomes acquainted with love and from which he receives his ethical nourishment. Here both conflicts and harmonies have educational value; a boy who has experienced common life with his sisters, a girl who has done so with her brothers, have gained unawares invaluable and irreplaceable moral advance as regards the relationship between the sexes. Over and above all, family love and brotherly love create in the heart of the child that hidden recess of tenderness and repose the memory of which man so badly needs, and in which, perhaps after years of bitterness, he will immerse himself anew each time a natural trend to goodness and peace awakens in him.

The Needs of the Political Commonwealth and Education

The second burden superadded to the normal task of education deals with the needs of the state and the political commonwealth in the postwar period. In this connection Professor Clarke, whom I have already quoted, warns us that "it is not for this generation to know the settled peace and quiet effectiveness of an assured and straight-moving education." He observes that the sense of amplitude and freedom enjoyed in so high a degree by his country's traditional education implied in reality the common acceptance, by the entire social environment, of strong and imperative mental and political patterns, of customs, habits, and standards deeply, subconsciously rooted. Thus the freest educational system involves in reality an authoritative character, "least obvious," he goes on to say, "just when it is most complete and unquestioned; when it is so secure, so absolute, so all-pervading that it feels no need to be obtrusive."

It is clear that for the educational body as well as for the individual citizen, freedom, rights, and autonomy have responsibility, duties, and moral obligations as their correlatives. In a human commonwealth, freedom and authority are as necessary for one another, by virtue of the nature of things, as their occasional conflicts are inevitable in actual fact. Political authority, that right to direct and to be obeyed for the sake of the general welfare, political authority is not opposed to human freedom, but required by it. In contradistinction to despotic authority, which directs a man toward the private and individual good of his master, and which places the one directed in a state of servitude, political authority directs free men toward the good, not of the one who directs, but of the multitude as a whole, or of the body politic—a common good which is desired by each component of the body politic, insofar as he is a part of it, and which is to flow back upon each one. Political authority, which is naught without justice, requires by its very nature free obedience based on conscience and moral obligation. The power of compulsion is only an additional property, arising from the fact that this command of justice may be, and is often in fact, disregarded by some. But without genuine authority, that is, without the very right to be obeyed by virtue of man's moral conscience, this power of compulsion is but tyrannical.

These basic principles apply to groups and particular bodies as well as to the individuals in civil society. The edu-

cational body, to the very extent that it is free and autonomous, is bound in conscience to the common good. To the
very extent that it is entrusted with an all-important function in the common good, it is bound in conscience to feel
responsible toward the entire community, and to take into
consideration the requirements of the general welfare.
Political authority, in the broad sense in which I use the
word, has not only to protect the freedom of teaching but
also to guide it toward the good of the whole, as far as a
matter essential to the very life of the whole is involved.

Indeed, the time of anarchical freedom, which is but a
false freedom, is gone. The crucial point is to pass on to an
age, not of servitude, but of real and organic freedom. As
concerns education, this is not the moment to accept any
philosophy which would warp its true essence, but rather
to affirm and maintain this essence more than ever. I am
afraid the new insistence on authority, therefore, if it de-
parts from the unchangeable lines of the education of man,
may perhaps deviate toward rather despotical educational
philosophies.

Professor Clarke's definition of education, as the "self-
perpetuation of an accepted culture, . . . of a culture
which is the life of a determinate society," is only given in
terms of social qualities, and is not adequate. If an accepted culture is permeated with errors, cruelties, or slavery, the task of education is not to perpetuate it, but to
strive to change it. No doubt Professor Clarke would not
deny that; and when he approves of the statement by Professor Hocking, "Education must produce the type," he
approves too of the second part of the same statement,
"and it must provide for growth beyond the type." *

Yet this very formula, even with its additional correc-
tion, remains terribly biological and sociological. Doubt-

* W. E. Hocking, *Man and the State* (Yale University Press, New
Haven. 1926).

less because education is immersed in a given culture and conveys it to youth, it produces in actual fact an average cultural type—but without having chosen such a task as its aim. Its real aim is to make a man. If the type is wrong, to grow beyond the type will perhaps result in something still worse. Education should essentially aim not at producing the type but at liberating the human person.

The educational philosophy of the production of the type is naturally akin to the trend of thought of Plato's *Laws;* for Plato the type must be produced by virtue of a "music" which is imposed upon education by the state. Modern states, especially modern states in the making, with their dependence on the masses and public opinion, and their crucial need of creating unity and unanimity in an emergency, will look upon such philosophy with special complacency. And they will take the application of this philosophy upon themselves. Then it would be no longer a question of Plato or of his *Laws.* The state would summon education to make up for all that is lacking in the surrounding order in the matter of common political inspiration, stable customs and traditions, common inherited standards, moral unity and unanimity, it would urge education to perform an immediate political task and, in order to compensate for all the deficiencies in civil society, to turn out in a hurry the *type* fitted to the immediate needs of the political power. Accordingly education would become a function directly and uniquely dependent on the management of the state, and the educational body an organ of state machinery. As a result of the extraneous and unnatural burden thus imposed upon education, and of the subsequent annexation of the educational task by the state, both the essence and freedom of education would be ruined. Such a process can succeed only with that utter perversion of the political state which is the totalitarian state, conceiving of itself as free from justice and as the supreme rule of good and evil. With a democratic state, this educational method would only lead to perfect disappointment. If the impact of the state upon education were conceived in this way, we should have to defend education against the state. In this connection it is not reassuring to read in the last book by so valuable and freedom-loving an educator as Dr. Meiklejohn the following statements: "Education is an expression of the will of some social 'organism, instinct with one life, moved by one mind.' Teacher and pupil . . . are both agents of the state." *

Yet the situation described by Professor Clarke remains undeniable. In normal circumstances, as he rightly points out, especially with strong aristocratic and traditional structures like those of England, the body politic regulates education less by way of the state than through the spontaneous influence of a stable and all-pervading social and cultural order. When this spontaneous regulation is lacking, the political body's regulation has inevitably to take place through state supervision. Such a supervision, nevertheless, should never imply any illegitimate interference of the state with the means and intrinsic norms of teaching. It should be strictly limited to those matters which directly interest the public welfare: the state might keep the educational body informed of society's needs for certain categories of activities and for the training concerned; above and over all, the state should see to it that no trend whatever opposed to the values which have been agreed upon as the very basis of common life and common fellowship may ever develop in education, and that the values in question should be carefully elucidated and firmly insisted upon.

Moreover peace, if peace is actually won, will be not a static but a dynamic and militant peace, which will require a tremendous effort of moral, social, and political reconstruction as well as of defense against the remainders of

* Meiklejohn, *op. cit.,* p. 279.

those egotistic and anarchical trends and that greed for domination which poison the world today. The freedom enjoyed by education, therefore, will not be a quiet and easygoing, peacefully expanding freedom, but a tense and fighting one. Yet while changing its mood and taking on a new and more stringent style, it can and must remain freedom. We may be sure that the educational system will not need any obtrusive pressure of the state in order to help the effort of the body politic toward moral unity. It will spontaneously coöperate, by sharing in the common inspiration. Democracies are aware today of their long carelessness in failing to defend and stress their own principles, their own intellectual and moral roots, in their own schools. They do not need to borrow totalitarian methods in order to remedy this lack. The great thing is that the democratic state itself have its own philosophy of life and society, and have faith in it. The generality of educators will be carried along on this faith, by virtue of good will or of conformity. Unity cannot be imposed by force and from without. Unity is but a result, as is peace, a result of actual inner inspiration, good will, and love for a common ideal clearly affirmed and a common task to be performed.

All of the new conditions I have mentioned may be satisfied without altering the essence of education. At any rate this very essence must remain intact. For the sake of the new civilization we are fighting for, it is more than ever necessary that education be the education of man, and education for freedom, the formation of free men for a free commonwealth. It is in education that freedom has its deepest human recess, where the reserves of freedom are kept alive.

The present war creates an immense need for technology and technical training. This need must obviously be satisfied, because of public emergency, while we maintain as far as possible the root exigencies of education. But after the war, however great the need for technicians may be, it would be an irremediable mistake not to return to the primacy and integrity of liberal education. Supposing that the training in liberal arts may be completed at nineteen, according to our ideal curriculum, enough time would remain thereafter for any intensive technical training, and this training itself should keep pace with that free and disinterested cultivation of the spirit which I emphasized apropos of the university period. For here we are confronted with the primary conditions of a community of free men.

3. THE EDUCATIONAL PROBLEMS RAISED BY THE PRESENT WORLD CRISIS OF CIVILIZATION

How to Remedy the Mental Perversion Brought about by "Education for Death"

Another category of problems is finally raised by the tragic conditions of today. I am referring to that perversion of human minds which is rampant in many parts of the world. German Nazism is the ultimate fruit of this perversion, and in its turn it spreads the latter throughout the world as a deadly disease. Once liberated, the peoples of the European countries now oppressed will be able to throw it off, be it at the price of temporary convulsions, if only their hopes and their will to revolt are not frustrated. Mental healing will be much more difficult in those countries which have been ravaged by Racist madness and Fascist dehumanization. Here the crucial question concerns Germany. We must have the courage to face the fact that the systematic cruelty displayed against the Polish, Russian, and other populations, the indescribable horror of the mass murder of millions of Jews, the scientific assassination of "useless" old or sick people in Germany, the very acceptance of letting loose the devil for the sake of a so-called patriotism and a so-called anti-Communist crusade, all these aberrations were not possible without a great many contributors and executioners sharing in the crime, and without a deep spiritual disease in large sections of the German people. We must face the fact that part of the German youth—those educated by Hitler for ten years— has been irreparably poisoned. Here we will be confronted after the war either with lasting perversion brought about by integral fanaticism, or rather with the total collapse and nihilism of minds helplessly disintegrated and devastated. Such a catastrophe is too great to make the idea of punishing an entire people anything but nonsense. The responsible ones must be relentlessly chastised. The people must be cured. This is not an easy or a rapid task. I shall not discuss here the remedies required from political medicine or surgery. What I am discussing is the preventive measures and the tremendous task of education needed.

Preventive or Protective Measures

Preventive or protective measures appear needed, because of that generation of German youth which has been intellectually and morally annihilated, and because, not only in Germany, not only in Japan, but in other countries too—even in democratic countries—there are men irremediably infected by what may be called the enslavement complex, which makes them sick of human dignity, mercy, justice, and freedom. If freedom is to live, is not the frenzy of slavery to be met with prophylactic action? In his book *How to Win the Peace,** C. J. Hambro states on the one

* C. J. Hambro, *How to Win the Peace* (J. B. Lippincott Co., Philadelphia and New York, 1942).

"In this field of national and international education, what we have called the peace intelligence service will have its first and most obvious task. The existing International Institute of Intellectual Cooperation with its network of Committees in practically every country must be reorganized and strengthened and establish its own peace patrol. Nations hand that with regard to the problems of our day nothing less comprehensive than a true world organization may bring the solution; on the other hand, that the primary necessity for a lasting peace is to maintain a sound intellectual and moral atmosphere throughout the world. He advocates therefore the primacy of the educational work to be achieved, and the formation of a "peace patrol" which would keep watch over the sources of possible moral epidemics and prevent such plagues as "education for death" from worming their way into any nation.

Let us not conceal the magnitude of the problem involved. Nothing is more risky than prophylactic measures in the realm of the human mind. Freedom runs the risk of being jeopardized by the very protective policy put into action for its own sake. And the modern world has at its disposal less dramatic but more effective means of coercion than the stakes of the fifteenth century. I dislike compulsion and I distrust world-wide mechanisms aiming at moral results. As a Catholic I know that even for a society divinely inspired such tasks of defense against imminent perils have their own perils too. Nevertheless in the face of such a mental disease as the one today spread over the world, we are forced to recognize the necessity of defending freedom and mankind by emergency measures, which moreover will probably prove necessary only for a relatively short time: for once the raging fever has abated, the hu-

have been united to fight dangerous drugs and have established a most successful organ of world-wide control. Spiritual dope . . . constitutes an even more mortal menace to mankind . . . A system of reports from national supervisory bodies to an international central board must be instituted. And this board must be coordinated with other organs of international control and power . . .

"Part of the work will be a superintendence of textbooks used in schools . . . Not only supervision of textbooks will be needed. It will be necessary to give schoolchildren an idea of world solidarity, international collaboration and the whole network of conventions and treaties which are the fibers of modern civilized life." (Pages 109, 112.)

man mind rather threatens to compensate for its former crisis of fanaticism by skepticism, as was seen in Europe after the religious wars of the sixteenth century.

Thus we might conceive of the "peace-patrol" which Mr. Hambro advocates as bringing the results of its inquiries before public opinion and before judicial agencies internationally instituted, in order to stop any propaganda and dissolve any school which inculcates sectarianism and intolerance, racial or political fanaticism, worship of hatred and enslavement. This peace-patrol would also prevent the granting of public office to any man who has been proved guilty of spreading the moral perversion just described. Such emergency measures should be concerned only with morality, without any political interference or *arrière-pensée*. They should moreover imply, as regards the agencies of the world organization in question, a mode of election and of functioning so balanced as to prevent any abuse of authority, and they should proceed with all the guarantees of law and juridical institutions for the suspected persons. Finally, with regard to the unfortunate German generation brought up under the empire of "education for death," it should be reduced as a rule to private life, with the exception of those individuals who would be proved to have resisted the evil and to be therefore capable of political or educational guidance. This should not depend on any discriminatory law against a category of citizens, but on a general program of psychological cure, valid for the period during which the United Nations will have to take care of the moral and material rehabilitation of the German population—a program concerned not especially with the generation in question but with the whole problem of healing the psychically disorganized parts of the population. The first step in such a program would be to have what the psychiatrists call a "clear area" serving as point of departure for the healing, and therefore to have psychologically and morally sound elements coming to leadership. The very leadership of these sane elements would prevent the insane ones from getting positions of political or educational guidance.

Constructive Work

Yet preventive or protective measures, however necessary they may be, are thoroughly insufficient, and the weakest of all. What is all important is constructive work, and positive inspiration. In this connection two main points ought to be made. First, if the present agony of the world means above all, as I believe, a supreme crisis of the Christian spirit, which for a long time has been neglected or betrayed in democracies, and which totalitarian states are now determined definitely to abolish, then it is obvious that a revival of Christian conscience and a new work of evangelization are the primary and unquestionable conditions for the moral re-education that the man of our civilization needs. If Western civilization thus rediscovers its root principles, even the Eastern peoples, with their own religiously minded civilizations, may avail themselves of the common awakening which would stimulate everywhere the naturally Christian trends of the human soul. The Christian mind has to cleanse itself of social prejudices due to historical sclerosis, and to become the quickening ferment of the temporal achievements of freedom. The democratic mind has to cleanse itself of materialistic or positivist prejudices due also to historical sclerosis, and to find anew its genuine spiritual sources in the Gospel inspiration. As concerns the German problem, the sufferings and faithfulness of many persecuted give promise of a religious renewal in Germany, which, if the spiritual flame remains free from any political or nationalist temptation, may afford, perhaps in the midst of dire internal conflicts, the chief motive power for a long and exacting moral reconstruction.

The second point deals with the large educational campaign which must be undertaken in the field of instruction. To heal reason which has been disintegrated by collective delirium and by the Nazi and racist cancer is not an easy matter. I am afraid that a swarm of professors sent from abroad as missionaries of true science would be given a rather cool reception by the German people and the other peoples of formerly Fascist states. It is more sensible to count upon the adaptability of the German mind and the deep reserves inherent in the peoples. The question will be to discover on the spot the elements capable of genuine intellectual leadership and to help them in their own way. The suggestion has been made that a particularly fruitful means would be the establishment of important international universities, notably in Central Europe, equipped with outstanding teachers and conceived as dynamic centers of intellectual radiance. These universities would not only give courses to students but also publish books and magazines, organize conferences and congresses in great cities, scatter lecturers everywhere, broadcast every day a large program of teaching directed to all parts of the population, and display every kind of intellectual activity.

The problem of the public schoolteachers, whom the Nazi regime has generally succeeded in annexing to barbarism, is an especially difficult one. For children must be educated, and such educators pervert children's minds. Many of these teachers should be dismissed and given other employments. Many others will probably manifest a sudden great zeal for justice and liberty. Not only should serious supervision be exercised, but an intensive work of enlightenment should be performed with regard to the entire body of public schoolteachers. Special schools should be created, preparing for their task new generations of teachers. All this should be subjected to the control of the supreme international agency of education, and even perhaps, during a period, to its direct initiative. It is likely that if a colossal work of reorganization of Europe and of the world is firmly undertaken, and if German peoples are given an idea of the role which the regenerated German mind may play in this work, they will accept more easily all measures of control and compulsion required by the moral as well as the political remaking of German countries. For they are ready to obey force, if it is for something great. What they will need above all is to be helped against despair.

Of course the positive work of education of which we are speaking is not to be limited to Germany. The whole world has an interest in it. And all men of good will should co-operate with it. Every cultural organization, and every group or association should be asked to contribute in some measure to the educational crusade. If half of the activity displayed by the Nazis for their disastrous propaganda were displayed for the good of education, the prospect would surely be hopeful.

About Europe

Since I am addressing an American audience, I should like to tell you something about Europe.

Let us not believe that to help Europe and re-educate it is an easy job. Europe is old and experienced, it has experience, a terrible experience, in wisdom as well as in wickedness. It has a deep sense of the tragedy of life, and a deep sense of what man really is. Neither idealistic formulas nor technological improvements mean much to Europe. It is now visited by death, starvation, the extermination of bodies, and the torture of souls, all the ordeals of the Apocalypse. It will be replete with bitterness. Europe, as well as Asia, will be sure to have learned a great deal and to know a great deal—a bitter knowledge of its own; it will have its own ideas and its own will as to the future of the world. Many dangers, such as the possible upsurge of nationalistic trends, of irreconcilable hatreds, of vengeful social resentments, will threaten its conscience. Perhaps the ordinary postwar phenomena of moral relaxation and I-don't-care-a-hang skepticism will take place in many people. But deeply rooted will be an abiding flame of revolt against the evils suffered and the injustices of the past. We must accept the risk of such a burning flame, which can be extinguished only by running a worse risk of moral chaos.

The point is to have this strong impulse directed toward an all-embracing constructive work and animated by a real sense of human rights and a real will to liberty and fraternity. The European peoples have their own way of looking upon this constructive work. They consider the particular features given to private ownership and free enterprise by capitalism to be already things of the past. And as a matter of fact Manchester liberalism is gone. Europe aspires to a new civilization, not to Communism, but to an order in which each human person may enjoy social as well as political freedom and the working classes reach their historic coming of age. Spiritually, the European peoples feel more or less obscurely that a new constructive impulse is possible only if Christianity frees itself from any encroachment by the human interests of ruling classes now morally bankrupt, and if Democracy frees itself from any blind and narrow dread of the Gospel values. In short, the oppressed peoples of Europe do not feel they need to be re-educated, they feel that they need to be liberated in order to coöperate with the Americas in the rebuilding of the world.

Such being the picture, we see what a huge effort of mutual adaptation lies ahead. If perchance the American people were to underrate the moral difficulty of the common task, or expected from distressed Europe that kind of tractability and prompt gratitude which the poor display toward the benevolent rich, or forgot that to bring one's love to the European peoples is also to put one's hand into a briar, my great fear is that by reason of disappointment and disillusionment this country might fall back into an isolation which would be a disaster for the world. Your ancestors left Europe and the oppression they suffered in order to create a new world for human fellowship and liberty. Now the time has come for you to turn your eyes back toward the old soil of sorrow and trial. The European peoples have always looked upon America as the Islands of the Blest. Be aware of the magnitude of the hope they have placed in you. They are not ungrateful, their anticipated gratitude is as great as their hope. If you give them only food and economic help and technical means, they will sincerely say "Thank you very much" and go about their own affairs. What they ask you to give them also is your trust. They ask that they be trusted in the things they are determined to undertake. The spiritual grandeur of the task in which you are engaged therefore must not be minimized. It is a task of heroic friendship. In other words, the first thing needed by all peoples is to share together in a common work which is greater than themselves and to which they truly give themselves, a common work both spiritual and material, and toward which the nations are now looking as the building up of a new Christian civilization. Europe and America have each their own ideas about this work, and their own conceptions about the internal economic regime suitable to each; while keeping their differences, these ideas may be adjusted, these conceptions may work together. No lasting good can be done to the world, if the sense of the tragedy of life, and that quality of heroism which Europe must display to overcome its tragedy, and the sense of the great human adventure, and that quality of heroism which America must display to lead her adventure to completion, are not joined with one another in boldness and faith.

May I quote you some passages of a prophetic page written in 1939 by that inspired and magnanimous Quaker scholar, Thomas R. Kelly? "One returns from Europe," he wrote, "with the sound of weeping in one's ears, in order to say: 'Don't be deceived. *You* must face Destiny . . .' An awful solemnity is upon the earth, for the last vestige of earthly security is gone. *It has always been gone,* and religion has always said so, but we haven't believed it. . . . One comes back from Europe aghast at having seen how lives as graciously cultured as ours, but rooted only in time and property and reputation . . ., are now doomed to hopeless, hopeless despair." * That sense of the tragedy of life, which has been the dire privilege of Europe, Thomas Kelly understood in his heart. And perhaps he died from it.

The second thing needed by peoples is mutual understanding. It is a pity to see how ignorant nations are of each other. When peace is made, and if some superior world agency of education is established, this agency should have a vast system of exchange-visits, scholarships, and grants organized in such a way that youths of all nations, and especially American youth and European youth, may acquire serious knowledge of their respective countries by sharing abroad not only in university life or social life but also in working life, farm and factory life. Knowledge gained by travel is most often deplorably superficial, and limited to the less representative or more deceptive social strata. The problem is to penetrate to a deeper level than

* Thomas R. Kelly, *A Testament of Devotion* (Harper & Bros., New York, 1941), p. 69. Douglas V. Steere, ed.

that of well-to-do folk, to share in the actual existence and concerns of the common people, and to discover their soul, not by criticizing and patronizing but by love. I am aware that the mental attitude of certain European travelers or even refugees does not correspond in this connection to the generosity of this country; as soon as they have landed many begin to criticize everything which differs from the cooking, habits, and methods of their own motherland. It is the reverse of this attitude that seems to deceive many American lovers of Europe. They often excuse everything or espouse the ideas and prejudices of the social circles which display for them their most attractive charms and civilities, and they sometimes disregard the real dynamism of that secret soil, of that soil of inner tension and conflicts which is the European soil. It seems that those among you who were the most indulgent to Italian Fascism or French Vichyism were those who had sojourned in France or Italy with the most affectionate feelings, and who, by dint of love for these noble countries, did not dare to abhor the very men and classes who betrayed the spirit of these countries, failing to perceive what was burning in the depths of the people itself.

The Renewed Inspiration of Our Own Education

I have discussed the work of mental healing which is especially needed by the people infected by Nazi education. But we must not forget that sometimes doctors themselves need to be cured. Nobody can give what he does not have. There are many deficiencies in the education of democratic countries; I have by the way pointed out what seems to me the principal ones in the course of these pages. A special danger is now to be mentioned, I mean the danger of an education which would aim, not at making man truly human, but making him merely into an organ of a technocratic society.

Of course, it is not a question of denying or belittling the immense need for technology which the present war has developed and which peace will also develop. This is a necessity which must be readily accepted. The question is to know the exact significance of technology for man, and not to transform technology into the supreme wisdom and rule of human life, and not to change the means into ends. This war is not waged for domination over men or even over matter. It is waged for liberty and justice, for equal rights, for releasing the onward movement of human history toward a commonwealth of free peoples; we are repeatedly told that it is waged for Christian civilization. All these are mainly spiritual values. What are we fighting for, if the only thing human reason can do is to measure and manage matter? If we have no means of determining what freedom, justice, spirit, human personality, and human dignity consist of, and why they are worthy of our dying for them, then we are fighting and dying only for words. If we and the youth who will be educated by future democracies hold everything that is not calculable or workable to be only a matter of myth, and believe only in a technocratic world, then we can indeed conquer Nazi Germany militarily and technically, but we ourselves shall have been conquered morally by Nazi Germany. For the preface to Fascism and Nazism is a thorough disregard of the spiritual dignity of man, and the assumption that merely material or biological standards rule human life and morality. Thereafter, since man cannot do without some loving adoration, the monstrous adoration of the totalitarian Leviathan will have its day. Technology is good, as a means for the human spirit and for human ends. But technocracy, that is to say, technology so understood and so worshiped as to exclude any superior wisdom and any other understanding than that of calculable phenomena, leaves in human life nothing but relationships of force, or at best those of pleasure, and necessarily ends up in a philosophy of domination. A techno-cratic society is but a totalitarian one. But a technological society may be democratic, provided this society is quick-ened by an inspiration which is supra-technological, and if it recognizes, with Bergson, that "the body, now larger, calls for a bigger soul," and that "the mechanical" sum-mons up "the mystical." *

Our crucial need and problem is to rediscover the natu-ral faith of reason in truth. Inasmuch as we are human, we retain this faith in our subconscious instinct. But we have lost it in our conscious reason, because erroneous philoso-phies have been teaching us that truth is an outworn no-tion and must be replaced by Kantian apriorism or other substitutes and finally by the feasibility of an idea, or the success of a process of thought expressed in doings, a mo-ment of happy adaptation between our mental activities and the practical sanctions. At the same time the universe and the reality-value of all that is not verifiable by sensory experience or humanly feasible have lost their meaning. With such a philosophy of pragmatism, a great thinker like Professor John Dewey is able to maintain an ideal im-age of all those things which are dear to the heart of free men; but outside of the ideological system, the historical impact of this philosophy upon culture will naturally lead to a stony positivist or technocratic denial of the objective value of any spiritual need.

We may thus understand by what internal conflict de-mocracy is now weakened. Its motive power is of a spiritual nature—the will to justice and brotherly love—but its philosophy has long been pragmatism, which cannot jus-tify real faith in such a spiritual inspiration. How, then, can democracy vindicate its own historical ideal—a heroic

* Cf. *Les Deux Sources de la morale et de la religion,* pp. 334–335; *The Two Sources of Morality and Religion* (tr. by R. A. Andra and C. Brereton), pp. 298–299.

ideal—against the totalitarian myths? "For that reason,"
as Dr. Meiklejohn puts it, "the day of pragmatism is done.
The movement which, for fifty years, has so gaily con-
signed older theories to oblivion because they were out-
moded, were out-of-date, is now itself open to the same
treatment. It, too, grows ancient. . . ." *

But the case of pragmatism is only one particular case
of a larger problem. In the last analysis, we have to consider the way in which philosophy has been challenged, not
by science, but by a masked metaphysics of science. Julian
Huxley is convinced that philosophical and religious asser-
tions are nonsense or useless hypotheses. And so they are
for him, it is true. Philosophers can understand the biological contributions of Julian Huxley, and recognize the
truth of biology as well as the truth of philosophy and religion, but I dare say Julian Huxley does not understand
our books and so feels firmly justified in denying philosophy all admittance to the field of knowledge. But philosophy is able to return the challenge. It indicts the very
method of such antiphilosophical scientists as inconsistent
with their own scientific method, and indeed rather naïve.
For they criticize philosophy and religion in the name of
science, which by their own confession has no knowledge or
criteria regarding such matters, and which might pass
judgment on them only on condition that it become philosophy. These men are in the same position as an auto-
mobile driver who would insist that planes are worthless,
because he knows how to drive and because to fly is not to
drive. To live in a state of doubt is a highly civilized attitude as regards the infinite potentialities and future con-
structions of science in its deciphering of phenomena. But
to live in a state of doubt as regards, not phenomena, but
the ultimate realities the knowledge of which is a natural
possibility, privilege, and duty for human intelligence, is

* Meiklejohn, *op. cit.,* p. 149.

to live more miserably than animals, which at least tend with instinctive and buoyant certitude toward the ends of their ephemeral life.

It is a great misfortune that both a civilization and education suffer from a cleavage between the ideal that constitutes their reason for living and acting, and that implies things in which they do not believe, and the reality according to which they live and act but which denies the ideal that justifies them. All modern democracies have suffered from such a cleavage. The task and mission of youth is to solve the problem at their own risk, to reunite real and ideal and make thought and action move as one.

Coming to the conclusion of this book, I think I may appeal confidently to American youth, because for a long time I have loved them as well as their great country. I should like to say to them: the world, which hungers not only for bread but for the freeing word of truth, the world needs you, it asks you to be as courageous in the field of intellect and reason as in the battles of land and sea and air. What your intellect and reason have to win is something which is not to be measured or manipulated by scientific tools but grasped by the strength of rational insight arising from what your eyes see and your hands touch; a universe of realities which make your thought true by virtue of their very being, and not merely as a result of successful action. This is the universe of intelligible being and of the sacred character of truth as such. You will then be able to show the world how human action may be reconciled with and permeated by an ideal which is more real than reality, and why it is possible and right to die for liberty.

As regards the prospect for education in America, I also should like to say that no story is more dramatic and hopeful, and testifies more strongly to the greatness of men of good will, than the story of the three hundred years of conquests achieved here, as told for instance in the book by Miss Agnes E. Benedict, *Progress to Freedom*.* The democratization of education, and the discovery, accomplished by dint of loving intelligence, of educational ways and means better fitted for the nature and dignity of the children of man, these constitute one of the glories of this country. Now it seems that American education finds itself at the crossroads. I am convinced that if it frees itself from the background of an instrumentalist and pragmatist philosophy which is but a hindrance to its inspiration, and which takes the edge off the sense of truth in our minds, this profoundly personalist and humanist educational venture will push forward with renewed power to a new work of pioneering.

* G. P. Putnam's Sons, New York, 1942. —I quote this book, because I read it with great interest and profit, and also because the very manner in which it joins a prejudiced and oversimplified philosophical background with a movingly generous, enthusiastic, and buoyant inspiration is a remarkable sign of the state of mind of many contemporary freedom-loving educators, who adhere to and foster lofty conclusions all the more ardently as they have been instructed in the pragmatist oblivion or rejection of the intellectual roots thereof.

INDEX OF PROPER NAMES

Adler, Mortimer J., 21 n., 70–72 n.
Aeschylus, 68
Alice in Wonderland, 49
Aquinas, St. Thomas, see St. Thomas Aquinas
Aristotle, 8, 11, 23, 30, 72 n., 95, 95 n.

Barr, Stringfellow, 64 n.
Baudelaire, 74
Benedict, Agnes E., 118, 118 n.
Bergson, Henri, 25, 85, 115, 115 n.
Blake, William, 74
Brubacher, John S., 7, 7 n., 17 n.
Bush, Douglas, 59, 59 n.

Calliope, 56
Cervantes, 68, 74
Cicero, 68
Clark, F., 93, 94 n., 97, 99, 101
Clutton-Brock, Sir Arthur, 23–24 n.

Dante, 68, 74
Demosthenes, 68
Descartes, 74, 82
Desert Fathers, 85
Dewey, John, 115
Donne, John, 74
Dostoevski, 68, 74

Eliot, Charles William, 65 n.
Emerson, 37
Epictetus, 68
Euclid, 31

Foerster, F. W., 20 n.
Freudians, 40

Gibbon, 68
Giotto, 74
Goethe, 68, 74

Greco, El, 74

Hambro, H. J., 104, 104–105 n., 106
Heard, Gerald, 40, 40 n.
Hegel, 74
Herodotus, 68
Hitler, 104
Hocking, W. E., 99, 99 n.
Homer, 68
How to Win the Peace, 104–105 n.
Hutchins, Robert M., 13 n., 23 n., 52 n., 54, 54 n., 65 n.
Huxley, Aldous, 40
Huxley, Julian, 116

Jefferson, 74

Kant, 32, 49, 52 n.
Kelly, Thomas R., 112, 112 n.

Lawrence, D. H., 74
Laws (Plato), 30, 100
Locke, John, 51

Madison, 74
Marcus Aurelius, 68
Marx, Karl, 74
Meiklejohn, Alexander, 60 n., 101, 101 n., 116, 116 n.
Michelangelo, 30, 74
Montesquieu, 68
Mozart, 52 n.

Nef, John U., 24 n., 47 n., 81, 81 n., 90
Newman, Cardinal John Henry, 51 n., 76, 76 n., 82
Nietzsche, 74
Nunn, Sir T. Percy, 51 n.

Orpheus, 56

Pascal, Blaise, 31, 68, 74
—— Étienne, 49
—— Gilberte, 49
Péguy, Charles, 70
Pestalozzi, 32
Phaedo, the, 29
Phelan, Gerald B., 75 n.
Pilgrim Fathers, 74
Pindar, 1
Plato, 29, 30, 48, 69, 84, 100
Plutarch, 68
Poe, Edgar Allan, 74
Posteriora Analytica, 72 n.
Progress to Freedom, 118

Quakers, 84

Rabelais, 20, 74
Racine, 68
Rights of Man, 74
Rousseau, 32, 74, 86

Saint John of the Cross, 85

Saint Paul, 11, 25
Saint Thomas Aquinas, 32, 50, 52–53 n.
Scholastics, 71 n.
Schopenhauer, 20
Shakespeare, 68
Sophocles, 68
Spencer, Herbert, 51
Spengler, Oswald, 84
Spinoza, 49
Steere, Douglas V., 112 n.

Tacitus, 68
Terence, 68
Thucydides, 68
Tolstoy, 74

Virgil, 68

Whitehead, A. N., 76–77 n.
Wilde, Oscar, 74

Zurbaran, 74